PLACE-NAMES IN THE
3000ft MOUNTAINS OF WALES

Front cover
Yr Elen is (most probably) named after a Celtic princess, a dream-girl from the south end of Caernarfon

Place-names
in the 3000ft Mountains
of Wales

by

Terence Ogmore Batt

ISBN: 0-86381-282-1

*First published on April 9th 1994 by Gwasg Carreg Gwalch,
Iard yr Orsaf, Llanrwst, Gwynedd, Wales.*

☎ *0492 642031*

Printed and published in Wales

I'm ashamed I don't speak the language myself
I'm told it's a grand language by them that knows

Old woman delivering the milk to Stephen Dedalus, Buck
Mulligan and the Englishman Haines at the Martello Tower,
Sandycove, Dublin, on Thursday 16th June, 1904,
in James Joyce's *Ulysses* (1922)

To Jac

Contents

Introduction

Snowdonia and Snowdon

The scenery in Snowdonia is the most spectacular in Wales. An early palaeogeologic submarine Ordovician volcanicity erupted violently on the scene from the sea-floor of a shallow sea once upon an ageless time long ago here in North Wales causing unprecedented devastation by volcanic detonation, landslip and earthquake, and, after a vast interval of time of land-mass and mountain-building, shaping and distortion, (an extraordinary change was near at hand in what had been up until then a warm and genial climate) intense quaternary glaciation then came with the successive incursions of the great Ice Ages, the latest long geological episodes in its history (when only the highest peaks just jutting out as nunataks were left uncovered by this massive crush of glaciation and glaciers), melted, and departed a mere ten thousand years ago. And it is this, this recent departure, that has profoundly affected the area and by its unremitting disfiguration produced the such spectacular scenery that we see today in Snowdonia. This remarkable range of landforms, unrivalled elsewhere in Wales, remains today as a vivid legacy of that latest Ice Ages' event. It still looks as though the glaciers retreated only yesterday. Mountains and moraine-dammed lakes and masterpieces of glacially-gouged-out suites of cirques and sharp arêtes and abysses of cliff and precipices and scaur and tumbled arrays of boulders and bare rock and sharp upright shards of splintered rock and crags and precariously perched erratics. This is Snowdonia. All this is very dramatic. It's the Ice what did it.

(Late Pleistocene Snowdonia, could we have walked in it eight or even nine thousand years ago, would be quite familiar and its present-day features easily recognised. This is Cwm Llydaw. That is Crib Goch. Crib y Ddysgl. Garnedd Ugain. Snowdon. Y Lliwedd. All look much the same. Yet we feel a sense of strangeness and unease about the pre-historic place for nothing

8

near at hand is quite 'right'. The lake is much higher. The vegetation around us is very different (we're in unbroken cover of a colourful woodland, the whole thickly-wooded valley filled almost to the summits with a canopy of deciduous trees). There must be red deer in this forest, wild horse, bear, wolf, boar and elk and auroch. There are hawks, falcons, eagles in the air. Soon no doubt there is destined to come a nomadic band of mesolithic Man. There *have* been changes of course since then but these are biological and recently historical rather than dramatically geological changes. In particular, the retreat of the Ice Ages triggered an interesting series of successions in the recent vegetational history of Snowdon's plants since the glaciers and this superficial botanical layer has been markedly modified more recently by latter-day Man.)

'Snowdonia' (a word which looks recently invented by an enterprising tourist trade to attract yet more caravans and cars and bed & breakfast visitors to this part of Wales) is not a modern word at all. The name goes far back. Legal documents in the Middle Ages were commonly inked in Latin and when Snowdon (then named 'Snaudun' or 'Snawdon') was referred to in the district's administration it was latinised as Snowdonia (or rather a likeness thereof, 'Snaudunia'). Then 'Snowdon' was synonymous with the areas we now call Snowdonia (though ever since the Normans the mountain itself began increasingly to assume its characteristic name). The name Snowdon was probably bestowed upon the region (*sic*), from a distance, by early 'English' passers-by because of its snow-covered appearance through many months of the year and because of its snow-line distinction, its elevation and extent. Ancient mariners on winter crossings across the icy waters of the Irish Sea and early travellers on trade and itinerary through less mountainous Wales no doubt both kept a respectful distant watch on the snow-covered mountains of North Wales, The 'Snow-Hills'. These forbidding and forsaken inaccessible fastnesses of Wales were the exclusive provinces of the unconquered Celtic 'Strangers', the wild Welsh. This was Snowdonia. The Region of The Snow-Hills. The Kingdom, by The Sea, of The Welsh. Snowdonia, for Anglo-Saxon and for the 'English', was definitely beyond the English pale. These mountain retreats were frequented only by the Welsh themselves. The mountains of Snowdonia played a not unimportant role throughout these crucial historical times in dictating the course and the outcome of many an event in the History of Wales.

Snowdon means The Snow-Hill. It is of course an exaggeration (a long-held fallacy) to claim (nowadays) that Snowdon holds a covering of perpetual snow throughout the year. Wales' firnline (2000 metres) is well above Snowdonia's highest peak (1085 metres). There are no glaciers now. There is not a year's-long retention of snow. But snow may fall quite heavily as late as June and return as early as September. The snow-bed frequently survives well into the summer in cracks and crevices on the north-facing cliffs of Snowdon, Carnedd Llywelyn, Ysgolion Duon and Y Lliwedd, disappearing only in late July in exceptional years. The average January temperature on the top of Snowdon is a chilling -5°C and much of the winter precipitation here falls as snow. Snowdon, then, is quite an apt name. It could well have been the nickname given by sailors (fishermen, whalers, merchants who plied their sea-trades along the Welsh and Irish coasts) to describe this mountainous array across North Wales when seen snow-covered in its winter raiment. Snowdon, most probably, is a seaman's name.

The early Welsh called this place **Eryri** which may have had the meaning of The Abode of Eagles (*eryi* in the ancient British language signified an eyrie or breeding place of birds of prey and *eryr* in modern Welsh means eagle). The old Welsh **Creigiau Eryri**, The Rocks of Eagles, was equivalent in meaning to our use of the word Snowdonia today. Snowdon (the mountain) was **Craig Eryri**, The Crag of Eagles. The place in medieval times must have abounded with birds of prey, *Falconidae* (falcons) and *Accipitridae* (eagles, osprey, kites, buzzards, harriers, hawks). It is a sadness indeed that the majestic golden eagle (*Aquila chrysaetos*) is no longer a part of the avifauna of Snowdonia. (Actually, on very rare occasions, an errant osprey or an eagle may re-visit the Carneddau and Glyderau in passing.) Snowdonian eagles no longer haunt

*The **Snowdon** range in characteristic winter raiment that probably gave the original Snowdonia its eponymic name. Snowdon means The Snow-Hill.*

*The **Snowdon** range across from Llynnau Mymbyr near Capel Curig*

these crags. Another olden name for the region in Welsh, **Creigiau'r Eira**, means The Rocks of Snow and this correlates well with the Anglo-Saxon expression 'Snaudunia'. Some Welsh scholars have linked the derivation of Eryri with the Welsh word *eira* (meaning snow) and this Creigiau'r Eira and suggest that Eryri originally meant (not The Abode of Eagles but rather) The Land of Snow. Perhaps, because *eryr* is also an archaic Welsh word (now obsolete) meaning boundary or edge, Eryri, simply, meant The High (The Mountainous) Land, The Edge. No-one now really knows. The Welsh today use Eryri to express a sense of Snowdonia parallel to the modern English meaning (meaning The Snowdonia National Park). Snowdon (the mountain) (or more accurately the very *summit* itself of Snowdon) is called in Welsh **Yr Wyddfa** (The Burial-Place, is one interpretation), **Yr Wyddfa Fawr** (q.v.).

Snowdon and Snowdonia are English titles now so deeply embedded in everyday usage that they have completely usurped and supplanted the old Welsh words for the mountain and the region. Snowdonia is an old word in Wales. But not as old as the Welsh **Eryri**.

Snowdonia was always a vague term, an uncertain kind of designation. For many it meant only that cluster of Snowdon, Glyder and Carnedd mountains in close proximity in Gwynedd whereas for others it later described all the general hilly and upland areas of the old counties of Merionethshire and Caernarvonshire (*sic*) and could even embrace the arm of the Lleyn (The Llŷn) Peninsula with its isolated monadnock hills. The modern-day notion of the word Snowdonia has now taken on a precise geographical meaning since definition of the (so-called) 'Snowdonia National Park' (**Parc Cenedlaethol Eryri**) (1951). The Half-Inch Ordnance Survey Map of The Snowdonia National Park outlines, at a glance, its extent and boundary in the newly re-named (post-April 1974) county of Gwynedd. But for most mountain-walkers and climbers who now come to Wales 'Snowdonia' continues to mean as it did once before that well-defined demarcation of mountain masses grouped together as the Glyderau, the Carneddau, the Snowdon Hills. The accompanying glossary remains true, in a retrospective kind of arrangement, in its geography, to this older sense of the word Snowdonia.

Welsh and Welsh Place-names

Wales (*When Was Wales?* is an unanswerable question to ask. 'Wales', the word itself even, is part of the traducing process whereby English legislators ignorantly skewed and created lasting havoc with Welsh place-names and patronymics (and likewise in Scotland and Ireland too). To those who speak the Welsh language there is no such entity as 'Wales'. 'Wales' is not Welsh. The land in which we live is called **Cymru**), Wales is a land with a uniqueness of landscape, language and culture. Wales' 'otherness' though, its essential 'difference', its 'separatedness' from 'England', is its possession of a distinctive and ancient language called Welsh. The vocabulary of Welsh is beautifully rich and resonant and powerfully evocative in its idiom and literature, its poetry and mythology. Place-names in Wales reflect and uphold this tradition.

Celtic-like languages were once widely spoken on the continent of central and southern Europe until steadily pushed to the Western Margins (Britain, Brittany, and Ireland). Welsh (like Breton and Cornish) belongs to the Brittonic (*Brythoneg*) branch of these early Celtic languages (with Irish, Manx and Highland Gaelic grouped within the Goidelic (*Goedeleg*) branch. Welsh as a distinct language emerged out of these marginalised beginnings and established itself within 'Wales' by the oral commonplace of everyday speech. It was the language of the common people and also of sage, poet, academic and magician. Welsh flourished with its Celtic embroidery of words used to narrate The Early Welsh Stories, those fabulous accounts of mystery, myth, tradition and legends. Welsh, written down, formed one of the earliest records of writing in what was otherwise an almost illiterate Europe. The language, **Cymraeg** (The Welsh Language), was literally the language of the people themselves, **Y Cymry** (The Fellow-Countrymen of This Nation) (The 'Welsh'-men) (United Against Their Enemy). These early Celtic settlers became an indigenous population of separate culture in Wales. Saxon invaders into Britain called these native Celts the 'Wealas' or 'Waelisc'. The Welsh. The Strangers.

The language was passed on orally from generation to generation and elaborated by professional poets and storytellers in Wales. It was a very 'cultured' society in its sense of the arts even though only a very few individuals could then read and write. Welsh was a spoken language and inevitably acquired over the centuries local idiosyncracies of speech and differently evolving folk-dialects, syntax and vocabulary, like any other language undergoing a process of natural transformation and change (it had to live, after all, side-by-side, with incoming Roman, Saxon, Norman, England). Then, in 1588, there appeared a momentous publication: a translation of The Holy Bible into Welsh by Bishop William Morgan (who was born in 1541 at a house called Tŷ Mawr in the hills above Penmachno). The Welsh Bible became at once a monumental literary resource not only for Welsh academics, bishops and poets but for the common Welshman and his family to learn by heart to read. Bishop Morgan's Bible provided by the outstanding accomplishment and quality of its linguistic excellence a standard written form of the Welsh language, the very best in Welsh vocabulary and idiom of Welsh expression. It is the rock of holiness on which the present Welsh language is so strongly built. It marks the sudden appearance of a cohesive standard language, Modern Welsh. Its publication without a shadow of doubt saved the Welsh language from degeneration and decay as Welsh weakened in the Celtic twilight with successive and recent invasions and incursions by the English.

Wales became overrun and ruled by the English. The 1536 Act of Union, in one outrageously insensitive surgical act without anaesthetic, 'incorporated, united and annexed' Wales to England. Economic and political coercion by the English, from the early sixteenth century onward, attempted to deliberately stamp out the Welsh language completely (the English succeeded with their extirpation of Irish, except in patches in places in the west and the remote western islands, the Irish-speaking areas, *An Ghaeltacht*).

Welsh was openly derided and prohibited as a medium for education and office in public life. The Education Act of 1870 made English the only language of instruction in Welsh schools and outlawed the use of Welsh in a child's education. A crude but effective punishment to stop Welsh children using their own language in class or in the playground was the enforced wearing of a token called the 'Welsh Not' (a placard hung around the neck), passed on from culprit to culprit until, at the end of the school day for whoever was last to possess it, a thrashing, a caning. Welsh was the first and only language of these children at home. The Welsh language was under great threat of complete loss by such systematic eradication. Welsh was spoken only in retreat by the hearth and at the chapel and in Sunday School. It only just survived. (Welsh family life in fact, and religion, saved it.)

Welsh quickly disappeared as a language spoken in childhood in schools in Wales and by the late 1950s in a grammar school in Glamorgan in South Wales lessons in learning Welsh held very much less interest for an intelligent English-speaking Welsh school-boy than learning Latin. Both were decidedly 'dead' languages but Latin at least had the great advantage of helping you understand long words in English all the easier. The situation for the Welsh language had become so desperate a decline that university students and otherwise respectable people (broadcasters, teachers, local politicians, ordinary householders in Wales) united in (unlawful) activities in the 1960s and early '70s (accompanied by a massive ground-swell of passionate opinion that gave them covert support) to safeguard the much-abused state of the Welsh language. This quixotic campaign undoubtedly did much to secure the present continuation and indeed the resurgence of interest in the Welsh language today.

The Welsh language today is still in great danger of further fragmentation, isolation, neglect and decay, but Welsh holds quite a remarkable record for its grip on survival. It is, in northern and western Wales, a truly *living* language with a most unusual resilience against outside intrusion and erosion that is possessed of a unique tradition, a distinctive culture, a fiery resistance and defiance, bilingual road-signs, bilingual policies in recruitment for jobs in education, in local authority administration, widespread publication in Welsh, Welsh-language newspapers and magazines, Welsh-only bookshops, *Radio Cymru*, transmission of the language and its culture through means of a television channel broadcasting to *thousands* of Welsh viewers through the medium of Welsh, *Sianel Pedwar Cymru* (Ess Pedwar Eck, S4C) (Channel Four Wales), several Welsh film units and studios, and the patriotic performances of Welsh rock-bands. The traditional health and future outlook of the Welsh-speaking Welsh is dependent not only on cymricizations like this and radio and television programmes and plays but, much more importantly, upon the strength and vitality and use of the Welsh language within the family circle, in shops, in the supermarket, in the work-place, within the local community, in the queue of the Unemployment Benefit Office. This is still the case in Gwynedd. Welsh is used quite naturally. This is the 'Welshest', Welsh-speaking, place in Wales. Many families in Gwynedd are bilingual with Welsh the only language spoken at home and also in school throughout childhood. The possession of Welsh is now a distinct advantage in seeking local employment in contemporary Gwynedd. Welsh, today, is the common language of the ordinary people in this part of Wales. And there are many good reasons why it should remain so.

There are over fifty million speakers of lesser-used languages in the multilingual, multicultural mosaic we call Europe, from Basque to Breton, Galician to Gaelic, Catalan, Occitan, Welsh and Irish, Romany, Lapp, Frisian and Faroese. Europe, even today, has a linguistic repertory of about a hundred tongues. Welsh makes it one hundred-and-one. Welsh is the mother-tongue of Wales.

Welsh, then, is Europe's oldest living Celtic language that is widely spoken. Five-hundred thousand, half a million or so, regularly speak the Welsh in Wales (with recent surveys indicating that at least a similar number again have at least some grasp on the spoken language). It is a rare and precious heritage from those early refugee Celts who came to the Island of Britain to settle in Wales. Newcomers to Wales may not know this. Road-signs and signposts clearly announce to visitors that Wales is still, today, a 'strange', a 'separate', a place apart. This is not 'England'. This is not 'Great Britain'. This is Wales. This is **Cymru**. *Croeso i Gymru*. Welcome to Wales.

Place-names in Wales are fascinating because many have meanings that proffer an accurately local description of the location itself or the topographical feature named or the natural history of its setting. Many Welsh place-names evoke in sound and in meaning a simplicity of great beauty within the Welsh landscape. This translates as often as not quite well from the Welsh into an equivalent (though corrupt and second-hand) English meaning. Most place-names are made up of easily remembered descriptive elements. The ninety-odd most commonly re-encountered on maps by walkers in the uplands and mountains of North Wales are listed below and each component Welsh word is given without complication a one-word English meaning. Welsh place-names often link these common elements in straightforward combination or in easily identified concatenation.

adwy	*gap*	**castell**	*castle*
afon	*river*	**cefn**	*ridge*
allt	*hill*	**clogwyn**	*cliff*
bach	*small*	**coch**	*red*
bedd	*grave*	**cochion**	*red (in plural)*
berfedd	*middle*	**coed**	*wood*
beudy	*cowshed*	**cors**	*marsh*
blaen	*head of valley*	**craig**	*crag*
bont	*bridge*	**creigiau**	*crags*
braich	*arm (spur of hill)*	**crib**	*ridge*
bron	*hill*	**cribin**	*ridge*
bryn	*hill*	**cwm**	*valley*
bwlch	*pass*	**ddôl**	*meadow*
cae	*field*	**ddu**	*black*
carn	*cairn*	**deu**	*two*
carnedd	*cairns*	**dinas**	*ancient hill-fort*
carreg	*rock*		*fortress-like rock*

dôl	*meadow*	**llyn**	*lake*
du	*black*	**llynnau**	*lakes*
duon	*black (in plural)*	**maen**	*stone*
dwy	*two*	**maes**	*field*
dyffryn	*valley*	**march**	*horse*
esgair	*ridge*	**mawr**	*large*
fach	*small*	**moch**	*pigs*
fawr	*large*	**moel**	*hill*
ffos	*ditch*	**mynydd**	*mountain*
ffridd	*upland pasture*	**nant**	*brook*
ffynnon	*well*		*river-valley*
foel	*hill*	**ogof**	*cave*
gafr	*goat*	**oleu**	*light*
gallt	*hill*	**pant**	*hollow*
garn	*cairn*	**parc**	*park*
garnedd	*cairns*	**pen**	*head*
geifr	*goats*	**perfedd**	*middle*
glas	*blue or green*	**pont**	*bridge*
gleision	*blue or green (in plural)*	**rhaeadr**	*waterfall*
goch	*red*	**rhiw**	*hill-slope*
gors	*marsh*	**rhos**	*moor*
graig	*crag*	**rhyd**	*ford*
greigiau	*crags*	**tal**	*front*
gribin	*ridge*	**tan**	*under*
gwastad	*plain*	**tri**	*three*
gwaun	*moor*	**twll**	*hole*
gwern	*marsh*	**tŷ**	*house*
gwyn	*white*	**tyddyn**	*smallholding*
gwynt	*wind*	**ty'n**	*smallholding (**ty'n** is a*
hafod	*summer dwelling place*		*contraction of **tyddyn**)*
isaf	*lower or lowest*	**uchaf**	*upper or highest*
las	*blue or green*	**un**	*one*
llan	*church*	**waen**	*moor*
llech	*slate*	**waun**	*moor*
llwybr	*path*	**wen**	*white*
llwyd	*grey*	**wyn**	*white*

y	*the, of the*
yr	*the, of the*
ystrad	*strath*

Welsh words are sometimes subject to changes both in spelling and in pronunciation through alteration, dependent on the immediate context, of the first letter of a word (this intentionally eases the flow of speech by avoiding too abrupt a change of tone-quality (*timbre*) in the voice in everyday conversation, but, to the ear of a 'foreigner' without the Welsh, it tends to make everything seem to slur into everything else when listening to the Welsh!). We enter here the quaking quagmire of the Welsh mutations (*Y Treigladau*) (under a wheeling of kronking crows protesting) where *c*, seemingly at random, can change to *ch* or *g* or a most improbable-looking beginning to pronounce, *ngh*, *m* mutates to *f*, and so mysteriously on into blank incomprehension. This makes looking up a version of a Welsh word in a Welsh-English dictionary particularly difficult, bewilderingly confusing for absolute beginners and frustrating even for advanced learners. Do not dismay. There is a regularity to these abstruse changes. Nine consonants (*b*, *c*, *d*, *g*, *ll*, *m*, *p*, *rh*, *t*) are mutable (at the commencement of a word in certain contexts) and may undergo one of three kinds of mutation: soft, nasal or spirant. Always look out for possible consonant changes. Double-check any seemingly unentered word in the dictionary against the following *Table of The Welsh Mutations*. This may help you track down an otherwise hopelessly elusive meaning:

Table of the Welsh Mutations

initial letter	soft mutation	nasal mutation	aspirate mutation
c	g	ngh	ch
p	b	mh	ph
t	d	nh	th
b	f	m	
d	dd	n	
g		ng	
ll	l		
m	f		
rh	r		

Most common among the place-name elements that keep recurring and repeating themselves in many a familiar place-name in the mountains of Snowdonia are **cwm, mawr** & **bach** and **glas** & **llyn** & **du**. Let's now look at each of these.

The Welsh Word 'Cwm'

Cwm is a well-known Welsh word meaning valley. Here in the context of the Ice Age-etched topography of Snowdonia (all this has been excavated and quarried and gouged out by the great abrasive advancing masses of established and retreating Ice), the word cwm is used to name and describe the location and the situation of huge amphitheatres and associated headwalls and high-placed upper-valley hollows on mountain flanks, the classic cirques, as well as the much wider valley floors which separate the sides of mountain from mountain. Remnant lakes may still remain in all these kinds of cwm. The Welsh word is embedded forever in the technical terminology of the geological literature as part of the descriptive nomenclature for a hanging valley (corrie or cirque). Cwm is pronounced as 'koom'. Do not make the embarrassing social solicism of pronouncing this word phonetically ('kqwim') which sound when voiced associates itself with an anatomical cleft or fissure, an altogether different kind of valley.

A valley familiar to many visitors is **Cwm Idwal** in the Glyderau. A far remoter valley in the Carneddau, **Cwm Caseg**, is entered only by adventurous walkers. And there is a valley high above the Llanberis Pass, seen by thousands of Snowdon Mountain Railway passengers, amusingly named **Cwm Hetiau**. All three, **Cwm Idwal, Cwm Caseg, Cwm Hetiau**, are cirques and each cwm by nature and by name is deserving of further description:

Cwm Idwal at the head of the Upper Ogwen Valley is now the most easily accessible (easy of access) mountain-valley in Britain. The geological structures and the natural history of Snowdonia are nowhere better illustrated than here. It really looks as though the glaciers retreated only yesterday. Cwm Idwal is a remarkable relic, a legacy of the last great Ice Age which left comparatively recently (geologically speaking) ten thousand years ago. There are erratics and moraines in evidence in abundance in Cwm Idwal. With so obvious a conspicuousness of glaciation and glacial retreat to be seen all round in Cwm Idwal, it's amusing now to note that when a promising student called Charles Darwin first visited the valley in 1831 with his professor of geology, Professor the Reverend Adam Sedgwick, examining the rocks for fossils, neither he nor his companion recognised Cwm Idwal for what it is and failed entirely to grasp the significance of the scenery all round them. The Ice Ages invested Cwm Idwal with a landscape whose impressiveness of geological features and botanical richness of rare relict arctic-alpine plants remains unsurpassed in this distinction elsewhere in Britain. (The rarest of the Welsh arctic-alpine flora is a small beautifully fragile plant called *Lili'r Wyddfa* in Welsh, *Lloydia serotina* in the scientific taxonomic nomenclature of Linnaean Latin, The Snowdon Lily in English. The inaccessible crags above Llyn Idwal in Cwm Idwal, and others elsewhere, have uninterruptedly provided a habitat for this rarity ever since the glaciers). Cwm Idwal in 1954 was declared Wales' first (and finest) National Nature Reserve. Cwm Idwal (this magnificent cwm) is renowned nowadays by climbers and walkers and geologists and ecologists conducting scientific investigation, and the like, just the same as once before, ages ago, when its changing and mysterious moods were revered and celebrated in the stories and writings of an emergent Welsh culture.

Owain Gwynedd, Prince of Gwynedd in the twelfth century, had entrusted his beautiful and very gifted child Idwal to a respected (but vain) academic called Nefydd Hardd (Nefydd the Handsome) to live safely in residence among the lakes and peaks around about Cwm Idwal and gain instruction in the arts of poetry and the harp. Nefydd himself had only a plain-looking and dull-witted son called Dunnawt, of Idwal's own age, and over the months the jealousy, envy and vanity of both foster-father and son against very good Idwal smouldered on until, by a wicked arrangement of complicity and insanity, innocent Idwal was led to the edge of a (39-foot) lake, flung in, and quickly drowned. The lake ever after this dastardly act has been a dark and gloomy place. From that time forth it has been called **Llyn Idwal**, The Lake of Prince Owain Gwynedd's murdered son, Idwal. It was believed in the past that no bird shall dare fly over its dark water as a result. You'll probably see lake-crossing birds crossing above Llyn Idwal's surface today, but obviously they haven't yet been told the lake's black legend.

(Idwal's brother Madog, a famous Welsh sea-explorer and another one of Owain Gwynedd's nineteen sons, sailed away one fine day from Porthmadog and, it is said, discovered America. Prince Madog landed on the shore of Mobile Bay in 1170, according to a plaque, and this of course was long before Christoph Columbus's Age of Discovery came. The Americas were only *re*-found by him, much later, five hundred years ago, in 1492.)

There is another legend about Cwm Idwal that tells of the burial here of a great Welsh giant, Idwal the Giant. His grave was the largest of several lake-side mounds and this can be discerned even to this day. Geologists, though, reckon this great hummock is merely another moraine, one moraine amongst many.

The sheer wall of cliffs at the stark back of Cwm Idwal was once known by local inhabitants as **Trigyfylchau**, an accurately descriptive Welsh name meaning The Three Adjacent Clefts. **Twll**

*The great north-facing ice-cut amphitheatre of **Cwm Idwal***

***Llyn Idwal** is a claustrophobic and gloom-laden lake
with a very black reputation*

Du (The Black Hole) (The Devil's Kitchen Cleft), that dreadful aperture and chasm, is the central cleft. The narrow and exposed path on the north cliffs (**Clogwyn y Gogledd**, The Cliff of the North, and **Clogwyn y Geifr**, The Cliff of the Goats) is rightly called **Llwybr y Geifr** (The Path of the Goats). The broader path at the south cliff (**Clogwyn y De**, The Cliff of the South) is described as **Llwybr y Carw** (The Path of the Deer). These natural and evocative Welsh names set within the amphitheatre of Cwm Idwal's headwall have largely been ignored on Ordnance Survey maps. The Welsh names of these paths and cliffs at Cwm Idwal's 'Devil's Kitchen or Twll Du', like many other absences from the maps, have been collected in the course of research for this work and are generously entered in **The Glossary**.

(The **Nant Ffrancon**, the whole extent of the Upper Ogwen Valley itself, is actually the true 'Devil's Kitchen', the 'Infernal Cauldron'. The name was given by sailors who in passing through the Menai Strait would often observe a turbulence of cloud, wraith-like at first, brewing up into a dark and evil-looking meteorology in that enclosed cauldron-like basin in the mountains we now call the Nant Ffrancon. *This* is The Devil's Kitchen. It was alleged to cause serious disturbance and error in navigation of the Strait. The valley was regarded more benevolently by the Welsh shepherd and drover who used it regularly as a safe retreat for his flock of sheep and herd of cattle though war and other conflict were afoot in Conwy, Bangor and Caernarfon. Few places in Wales could have been more difficult of access than Nant Ffrancon in olden times. Nant Ffrancon is now a lake-less infilled green alluvial plain though it once held a great blue glacial lake nearly three miles in length, **Llyn Glas Mawr**, mistakenly called **Llyn Ffrancon**, which had silted up long before the arrival of those freelancing foreigners, the Teutonic mercenaries, The Franks, from whom the valley, Nant Ffrancon, takes its name.)

Cwm Caseg is a remote place in a recess deep within the enormous upland ranges of the Carneddau. The name means The Valley of the Mare. Legend tells that the half-wild ponies of these mountains come each year in spring to this most secret of valleys to

*A cleft, an aperture, a chasm in the cliffs at the back of Cwm Idwal. This is the dread **Twll Du**.*

foal beside **Ffynnon Caseg**, The Mare's Well, beneath the enclosing cliffs of Carnedd Llywelyn and Yr Elen. The legend of Cwm Caseg as the birth-place of the mountain ponies which roam unattended in the uplands and moorlands of the Carneddau, quaint though it sounds, is in fact an old tradition that comes very close to being true. It is an accurate observation of upland natural history.

Cwm Hetiau is positioned high above the Llanberis Pass in **Cwm Glas Bach** (The Small Green Valley) and has an amusing explanation to its historically recent name. I relate the story of

Cwm Hetiau like this. Clogwyn Platform on The Snowdon Mountain Railway is such an exposed station at such high elevation on the mountain that the windflow on the platform is unimpeded. Passengers alight here to see the village of Nant Peris two thousand feet below and peer down from this unprotected stop with evident trepidation into the abyss of Cwm Glas Bach below. Victorian tourists wore expensive headgear. Hats were blown away from here quite regularly, by astonishingly sudden gusts of wind, to tumble headlong into a craggy and inaccessible valley far below, Cwm Hetiau. But astute locals benefited by such mishap. Villagers from Nant Peris would cheerfully come up at weekends to gleefully recover from Cwm Hetiau, briskly collect, many a basketful of hats and other head-dress whisked away by the wind from the heads of those hoity-toity English tourists. More than one quarrymen showed off his newly acquired black bowler hat to admiring colleagues at the slate quarry next Monday morning. Doffed it like a toff he did. The name remains, on our Ordnance Survey maps, **Cwm Hetiau**, which in English means 'The Valley of the Hats'.

Mawr & Bach

Mawr and **bach** mean great and small respectively, though when these adjectives are suffixed in the Welsh to the common (shared) names of attached mountains, adjoining valleys or close-lying lakes the meaning is not absolute but rather invites our relative comparison of the two (*mawr*: the higher in height, the greater in surface area or extent; *bach*: the lower in height, the smaller in size or extent). **Glyder Fawr** and **Glyder Fach** are the two mountains with distinct tors and outcrops of rock set some distance apart on the lunar-like landscape of The Glyders, *fawr* and *fach* (mutations of *mawr* and *bach*) indicating the higher (3279 feet) and lower (3262 feet) in height. **Marchlyn Mawr** (The Stallion Lake the Greater) and **Marchlyn Bach** (The Stallion Lake the Smaller) are two lakes close at hand in the Glyderau under **Elidir Fawr** (3030 feet) and **Elidir Fach** (2565 feet) which names themselves need no further

A mountain-pony and her foal in spring at the entrance to **Cwm Caseg,**
The Valley of the Mare

The headwall of **Cwm Caseg** *and the oligotrophic lake* **Ffynnon Caseg,**
the water of which, who knows, may give easement in equine parturition

explanation. **Ceunant Mawr** and **Ceunant Bach** refer to The Great Gorge and The Lesser Gorge. **Cwm Glas Mawr** is The Large Green Valley and **Cwm Glas Bach** is The Small Green Valley.

There is an interesting exception to the usual accuracy of the designations *mawr* and *bach* in the mountains, and this is found in the northern Carneddau hills. There are two clusters there of outcropping rock not too dissimilar in appearance or size, **Bera Mawr** and **Bera Bach**. But Bera *Bach* (The Rick of Rocks, The Stack, the 'Lower', the Lesser), is the *higher* positioned of the two outcrops at 2648 feet. Bera *Mawr* (The Rick of Rocks, The Stack, the 'Higher', the Greater) is definitely the *lower* stack at 2605 feet. The great rocks called Bera Mawr probably acquired the 'higher' or 'greater' emphasis and status because of this stack's sole prominence of position and apparent highest elevation when seen from the usual view and approach to the northern Carneddau, at Aber Falls, and the discrepancy only much later revealed by ordnance survey. This came too late to change the names. Perhaps. Whatever the explanation, the names Bera Mawr and Bera Bach remain in isolated exception, an odd anomoly, here in the Carneddau. Elsewhere in the mountains, *mawr* means the greater and *bach* means the lesser.

Glas & Llyn & Du

Glas translates variably as green or blue or a sheen or shade betwixt and between blue and green, pale, or grey, and in Old Welsh **glas** could also mean stream. **Llyn** (pronounced as 'thlin') means lake. **Llyn Glas** (The Blue Lake) in **Cwm Glas** (The Green Valley) is a charmingly tranquil little lake with its two-tree'd ait cupped on top of a massive shelf of rock in a remote and quiet place high above the Llanberis Pass. Glas and llyn combine to name **Glaslyn**, a bottomless lake under the sheer cliff-face of the east precipice of Snowdon. (Quite a few of Snowdonia's lakes were deemed 'bottomless' until the age of scientific enlightenment arrived, a

Glaslyn *from Crib Goch*

century or so later here than elsewhere, when Glaslyn, at a height above sea-level of 1970 feet, was sounded by plumb-line to a depth of 127 feet of water.) Glas quite accurately describes the colour of Glaslyn's water. It is indeed The Blue (Green) Lake. This lake is the dramatic source of the **Afon Glaslyn** (The River Glaslyn). Two hundred inches or more of rain is on average the annual rainfall recorded on Snowdon (There is obviously some justification for North Wales' reputation as a destination with constancy of rain. This is good news at least for lakes and waterfall-watchers. And, anyway, water (*passim* in Wales), *dŵr* in Welsh, water is, after all, the greatest ingredient of all good legends), and this collects at first in Glaslyn. The text now follows the flow of the Afon Glaslyn from its outflow at Glaslyn and encounters on its course, in turn, **Llyn Llydaw, Llyn Gwynant** and **Llyn Dinas** . . .

Llyn Llydaw is a great lake. It, like Glaslyn, is remarkably blue. The intensity of its tint of blue seems almost too blue to be true, but in fact the lakes are indeed coloured this colour by the leaching out of copper ions from the mineral-rich rocks hereabouts. Copper mining has certainly taken place here since, well, since at least the time of the Roman Occupation. The Miners' Track (**Llwybr Mwynwyr**) was laid in the mid-nineteenth century and the copper miners' causeway (**Y Cob**) was constructed by the Cwm Dyli Rock & Green Lake Copper Mining Company as a short-cut across Llyn Llydaw to more easily reach mine-workings and buildings (like **Y Felin**, The Ore-Crushing Mill beside Llyn Llydaw). These were once industrial and active copper mines. The site is abandoned and derelict now. The main Britannia Copper Mine ceased activity (resuscitated briefly in 1915 as The Penypass Copper Company) and closed in 1916. The forsaken and forlorn dis-used ruins of the buildings and miners' barracks decay by the lakes.

Llyn Llydaw is translated as Brittany Lake. But there's something very wrong about this 'Brittany Lake' in Snowdonia. Brittany (or Armorica by its old name) is the north-west peninsula of France. It's out of place in a place like this. It grates and goes against the ubiquitous Welsh tradition of naming a place with a simple yet accurately descriptive name in the Welsh that identifies its local identity. I don't believe it at all (though it's satisfyingly appropriate that this so-called 'Brittany Lake' outflows into **Cwm Dyli** which when translated literally means, mischieviously, The Valley of Stupidity or Nonsense!). The name of the copper-mining company 'Britannia' is easily corrupted to 'Brittany' by the untutored speech of incoming mining adventurers and mine-managers' and the pun, the joke of the thing of course, is that the word 'Llydaw' (Brittany in Welsh) then relates to the Britannia Copper Mining Company itself. No, 'Brittany Lake' is *not* the meaning of Llyn Llydaw's original name in the Welsh.

There really is no clear-cut translation for Llyn Llydaw. Some authorities in these matters claim that *Llydaw* is a corruption of the

Llyn Llydaw from Bwlch Ciliau

Welsh word *llydan* meaning broad or wide. Others think that *Llydaw* is derived from *lludw* meaning ashes, a reference perhaps to the refuse of copper smelting or to the natural occurrence of cinderlike rocks and ashy material along the lake's shore. *Llydaw* has also been translated as coastland (extending along the water's edge) hinting at a link with evidence of a settlement of lake-side dwellings and the discovery during a partial draining of the lake of a primitive wooden skiff or canoe (an oak logboat) buried at its bank. Perhaps *llydaw* is simply a proper name, the name of an important person living near the lake in an ancient time. There is no clear-cut translation for Llyn Llydaw.

Llyn Llydaw is a great lake. It is 190 feet deep. It is *The* Great Blue (The Great Green) Lake of Snowdonia. It may not be accident but insight that in giving the lake this honest and simple description we are now only a linguistic tongue-trip or two away in pronunciation from Llyn Llydaw ('Thlin Thlud-Dow'). This Great Blue-Green Lake in Welsh is **Llyn Glas Mawr**. Do not confuse this with its namesake transient lake in the Nant Ffrancon, another (even greater) Llyn Glas Mawr.

Llyn Llydaw (The Great Blue-Green Lake) outflows into **Cwm Dyli** (The Valley of a Great Flow of Water) and the still eagerly youthful Afon Glaslyn gambols and tumbles and cascades and waterfalls its way down into the valley of Nant Gwynant. It used to. This once great flood (a deluge of rushing water) is now considerably diminished by the diversion of Llyn Llydaw's great reservoir of water at **Cwt Falf** (The Valve-House) into a notorious and ugly out-of-place eyesore in this otherwise very pretty part of The Snowdonia National Park, **Pibell Dŵr** (The Water-Pipe). The National Power Pipe-Line. For watts. For the generation of an unashamedly meagre amount of hydro-electric power. The Afon Glaslyn carries on to **Llyn Gwynant**.

Llyn Gwynant nestles in Nant Gwynant, and an older name for this beautiful valley was **Nanhwynen** (**Nant Gwynen**) meaning The Valley of Gwynen (Gwynan, Gwynain), a personal name. It is unlikely then that Llyn Gwynant means anything like The Lake of the White Brook or The Lake of the White (Untainted, Pure, Unblemished) Little River or The Lake of the White (Pure, Holy, Hallowed, Revered) River Valley (The Perfect Valley Setting), and however attractive this looks as a written description for the lake it would nevertheless be a most deceitful act of translation to suggest it has this kind of meaning. Anyway, such words only inadequately describe the natural perfection of Llyn Gwynant's situation. The lake is best viewed from view-points on the Penygwryd to Nantgwynant road. You could say with truth that the entire Snowdonia National Park can have nothing else to show the casual visitor more remarkably beautiful and perfect a view than Llyn Gwynant in this setting. It's very pretty.

Llyn Gwynant nestling in Nant Gwynant

Llyn Dinas means The Lake of the Hill Fort Place, in reference to a nearby oak-wooded crag, a natural fortified position from long ago, **Dinas Emrys**. This dome-shaped emplacement became the stronghold of the post-Roman leader known as Ambrosius, called Emrys by the Welsh, brother to Uther Pendragon, the father of King Arthur himself, and hence its name, The Fortress of Emrys. Disturbance and darkness had descended on the land with the decline and withdrawal (The Fall) of the Western Roman Empire. The marvellous boy Merlin was sought and brought before Ambrosius. The story then tells of young Merlin's awakening at Dinas Emrys of two underground dragons, The Red Dragon (**Y**

Ddraig Goch) (signifying Wales) and The White Dragon (symbolising the usurping English) (*Saeson*, Saxons). 'Twas by all accounts a long and a terrible fight to behold between The Two Dragons of Dinas Emrys ('a-scratching and a-tearing of dragon-flesh from body and bone with flailing claws they did fought') (dragons, serpents, griffins, snakes, water-beasts, witches, magicians, physicians and giants were but a few of the strange medieval creatures which once inhabited North Wales). It is reassuring however for those of us living in Wales that the story in its prophecy declares that eventually (The Welsh, you see, will never surrender) The Red Dragon won. The symbolism of the Dinas Emrys dragon-story developed into the banner and emblem of the Welsh and Wales. The Welsh flag. The figure of The Red Dragon on a green and white background. The Red Dragon is fissilingual. The Welsh Dragon has two tongues. The Red Dragon won.

(**Sais**, Saxon, though it now means an Englishman, remains a term of abuse in Welsh. *'Blwdy Sais'*, mutters an aggrieved Welshman under his breath and then utters an obscene oath in Welsh, *'Iechyd da pob Cymro, twll din pob Sais'*, an imprecation which means 'Good Health to All Welshmen, (Something Nasty and Scatological) to The English'. But, *chwarae teg, mun*, the very word 'Welsh' itself, until very recently, was a pejorative expression in the English language. In my *Thesaurus of English words & phrases*, 'welsh' is cross-indexed with the words abscond, run away, elude, defraud, not pay. There always has been this internecine distrust, this mutual animosity, between the English and the Welsh.)

Merlin later became King Arthur's personal counsellor and consultant magician. Amidst a mostly illiterate population, any well-read man like Merlin who experimented in science and medicine would have been thought a magician. Merlin, after all, had a good collection of books. Merlin, though, was different. Merlin was not only a worker of scientific wonders, a sorcerer, a wizard, but also a great soothsayer too (but called behind his back, by the Welsh, **Myrddin Wyllt**, Merlin the Mad, though also

Dinas Emrys, an unassuming little oak-clad hill-crag under a shoulder of Snowdon

Dinas Emrys has excellent vantage over entry into Nant Gwynant and overlooks for the most part its namesake lake, Llyn Dinas

known more respectfully as **Myrddin Emrys**, Merlin Ambrose, The Great Enchanter). Merlin Emrys lived at Dinas Emrys. Merlin (using a bit of magic and assisted no doubt by a few local miscreants) moved in and occupied for some time the top of this outcrop after playing a practical joke on its most recent occupant King Vortigern (Welsh-born Gwrtheyrn), that unhappiest of all British Kings. (King Gwrtheyrn had exasperated and infuriated his own people by ingratiating himself with the detested Saxon invaders, letting them in. He hurriedly retired to Dinas Emrys.) Dinas Emrys became Merlin the Magician's impregnable position (until that is he took for apprentice a certain sister-enchantress called Morgana le Fay, but that's altogether another legend). The sheer and inaccessible valley of **Nant Gwrtheyrn** (The Valley of Vortigern), on the north coast of the Llŷn, was the last hiding-place of King Gwrtheyrn. Merlin, in time, became well-respected by the Welsh as their very own and everlasting legendary medieval Welsh Magician.

The bare historical fact of the matter is that the outcrop known as Dinas Emrys began as an Iron Age hill-fort and this remained occupied throughout succeeding Ages as a position which afforded an excellent look-out place that had vantage over entry into the pass at Nant Gwynant. It overlooks for the most part its namesake lake, **Llyn Dinas**.

The River Glaslyn flows on from Llyn Dinas past Dinas Emrys down to the stone-cottaged village of Beddgelert, (This is not the place to tell (or re-tell) (or discredit and expose the tourist-attracting pan-European fiction) (of) the apocryphal story of the grave (*bedd*) of Gelert (*Gelert*) (the faithful but dead dog) (of) (slain by) (an overly-hasty though ever-afterward truly remorseful Prince Llywelyn) (it is after all too good a story to disbelieve) other than to say that it (the legend) (the dog) is a local villagers' invention from the late eighteenth century, plotted by one David Pritchard, shrewd innkeeper of The Goat Inn, Beddgelert, to contrive to attract more pilgrims and the like to pass that way. The village ever after prospered. Beddgelert, because of this maggot, is today a thriving (crowded) North Wales' tourist attraction. But the name

Beddgelert, no matter how heart-rendingly is told the tale, does *not* mean The Grave of the Faithful Hound Gelert. Beddgelert is definitely not Dead-Dog City. **Beddgelert** in fact rather than fiction means The Grave of Saint Celert (Hermit-Saint Celert ap Math) who had established a cell at the site in the sixth century on a bank of the passing Afon Glaslyn which) gains strength, rushes and tumbles its way in a hurry through the Pass of Aberglaslyn (The Confluence of the Glaslyn, The River-Mouth of the Glaslyn) under **Pont Aberglaslyn** (the bridge where the River Glaslyn once reached the high tide of the sea), and then thereafter slowly flows on a slow course, leisurely, meanderingly, recently, to the embankment-held present-day position of the sea. Cardigan Bay. The best parapet to stand to watch the now broad and winding Afon Glaslyn cross **Y Traeth Mawr** (The Great Shore) (The Great Land Reclamation Strand of 1811) is that at **Pont Croesor** (The Bridge to the hamlet of Croesor). It is overlooked by a highly photogenic angle of **Cnicht** ('The Matterhorn of Wales') (The Hill, The Knight's Helmet, The Icicle, The Knight) and the two **Moelwyns** (The White Hill Summits) (**Moelwyn Mawr** and **Moelwyn Bach**). On the down-stream side of the bridge the river departs for **Porthmadog** (The Port of Mr William Alexander Madocks) (The Harbour of Departure of legendary Prince Madog who sailed away from here to discover America). This river has had an eventful journey (there is even an Open University programme about it called *From Snowdon To The Sea*) that began with its unrivalled origin under the intimidating and often rain-sodden cliffs of Snowdon, there in the far distance, at **Glaslyn**. The Blue-Green Lake.

By the (the riparian) (the lacustrine) way. An enormous water-beast, the monstrous **Afanc**, lives in the depths of Glaslyn. This is its reluctant residence since being forceably evicted from causing more mischief and malice when the Beast lived in its former home, a river-pool called **Llyn yr Afanc** (The Pool of the Water-Monster) near **Betws-y-coed** (The Chapel in the Trees) where its depredations (frequent floods, ruined crops, drowned cattle) had become a bleedin' public nuisance. Tricked from its lair by the prettiest of allurements, a beautiful young maiden bathing half-undressed by the river-bank who acted out a most enchanting fifteen year-old decoy in this deception, the Afanc (with complete disregard for social courtesy in courtship of the girl) straightaway rested its ugly amphibian head on the young girl's lap and laid one of its huge webbed claws, gently, on the softness of an innocently exposed adolescent breast. The cunning trap was sprung. The local citizenry dashed out from hiding in the trees and threw coil after coil of heavy chains around the beastly body of the Beast. The Afanc violently recoiled from the attack (ripping off with its clenched claw the poor lass's left breast, a singularly messy sort of unilateral masectomy, poor girl) but the chains held true. The Beast was chained in capture. A pair of mightily strong long-horned oxen were attached to the bellowing bundle and the enraged beast was dragged protesting down the Lledr Valley and over the western shoulder of **Moel Siabod** towards its distant destination, Glaslyn. The effort of the haul at **Bwlch Rhiw'r Ychen** (The Pass of the Ascent of the Oxen) caused an ox's eye to drop out and the flood of tears it shed formed **Pwll Llygad yr Ych** (The Pool of the Ox's Eye). The water-monster was released into the barren depth of Glaslyn in banishment high up in the mountains, out of harm's way in exile, and little has been seen of it ever since then. But it is said that the Afanc is still alive and the ageing beast ('toad-like with tails & wings, and shrieks') has been known to feed on the unsuspecting toes of disobedient little children who paddle out too far from Glaslyn's shingle shore against parental advice. The Afanc of Glaslyn awaits.

Llyn means lake and **du** means black and du and llyn combine to name that dark deep lake in the Carneddau at the edge of nowhere in the middle of nowhere, **Dulyn**, The Black Lake. Dulyn is 189 feet in depth. At the base of **Craig y Dulyn** (The Crag of the Black Lake) (The Cliff-Face Precipice of Dulyn) a sounding has shown a depth of 55-foot of water at a distance of only 3 feet out into the lake. Dulyn is also the Modern Welsh for the fair city of Dublin (where the girls are so) and 'Dublin', in modern-day English, means Black Pool (Dublin in the original Irish (Erse) was (and is)

Glaslyn, The Blue-Green Lake, under the east face of Snowdon. The reptilian Afanc of Glaslyn awaits.

Dulyn, The Black Lake, under the dark precipice of Craig y Dulyn. This bottomless lake is at the exact geodetic centre of the Carneddau.

Daile Átha Cliath, Ford of Hurdles Town), **Dulyn** (the lake in the Carneddau) is probably better translated as The Black Pool. Translation is never a straightforwardly literal act. Even words like *glas* and *llyn* and *du* are not as innocent as at first they seem. Many difficulties await.

More and More Difficult Names

So, many Welsh place-names are a simple assembly of easily remembered descriptive words whose meaning can be looked up in a vocabulary list even as short as a hundred common elements, as above, and this kind of translation often 'cracks' the approximate or even the apodictic meaning of many a place-name in Wales. Most guide-books to walks in the hills and mountains of North Wales and other publications on the geology, history and natural history of Snowdonia, in English, are well-intentioned in this respect in providing a page, a 'glossary', of Welsh place-name elements. This works well on occasion, 'explaining' names like **Cwm Glas Bach, Cwm Glas Mawr, Crib Goch, Bwlch Glas, Afon Glaslyn, Nant Ddu, Nant y Graig, Tŷ Gwyn, Afon Gafr, Twll Du**, but this casual kind of do-it-yourself interpretation (with its inherently false assumption of an exact equivalence of a Welsh word with only a one-word English meaning) proves at best only superficial (and generates 'explanations' badly in error sometimes, illiterate, ridiculous distortions, which then may independently begin to perpetuate themselves in print).

The more persistent enquirer will soon discover the inadequacy and insufficiency of the guide-book's glossary or any such limited vocabulary list as this and so turns to consult the pages of a Welsh dictionary (pocket-sized or otherwise), aware all the time of the awkward complication on occasion of needing to compensate for *Y Treigladau*, to look up the meaning of place-names like **Cwm Caseg, Cwm Hetiau, Clogwyn y Person, Crib y Ddysgl, Pant yr Lluwchfa, Bwlch y Saethau, Bwlch Cyfrwy-drum, Bwlch Eryl Farchog, Ffos Pantyrychen, Drws Nodded, Llyn y Caseg-fraith, Y Gwyliwr, Y Galan**. The less diligent will abandon the search for

Cerrig Cochion, Creigiau Gleision, Castell y Geifr, Gwaun-y-gwiail, Foel Meirch, Ysgolion Duon, Cwm Cesig, Cwm Treweunydd, Cwm yr Hyrddod, Llyn Nadroedd, though the serious researcher will soon become accustomed to recognising any such pluralities as these. But, after this, then the real difficulties of translation begin . . .

There remains a bothersome hard core of place-names too 'difficult', too obscure, for an 'easy' translation. The dictionary, now, is of little or no avail. Too troublesome to try elsewhere to trace. They will taunt and defy undeciphered on the map, a mystery as to meaning. Names like **Cwm Dudodyn, Cneifion Duon, Nant Ffrancon, Llyn Ogwen, Llynnau Mymbyr, Cwm Cowlyd, Llyn Eigiau, Llwytmor, Gledrffordd, Drosgl, Yr Aryg, Maen Trichwmwd, Carreg Minianog, Tryfan, Bwlch ym Mhwll-le, Afon Gwyrfai, Cwellyn, Gwastadannas, Allt Maenderyn, Yr Aran, Cwm Tregalan, Chwarenog, Clogwyn Du'r Arddu, Ynys Ettws, Dinas Mot, Penygwryd, Nant Gwynant**. 'Difficult' names like these are not uncommon (even a name of innocent appearance, like Nant Gwynant, a barbarism of modern origin, may be bristling with unexpected difficulty in translation) and without independent guidance and other helpful assistance the inquisitive walker, curious to know all place-names' meanings on a walk (most walkers are expert map-readers, but only a handful are anything but uninitiated amateurs in following this kind of translation), soon becomes hopelessly 'lost'. The names will otherwise remain unknown in meaning.

There is of course the need for the publication and general availability of a comprehensive and 'definitive' *Glossary of Welsh Place-Names in The Mountains of North Wales*. The present work sets out to achieve this. Or at least to act as a guide and beginning for others to follow.

A central challenge to the satisfactory completion of this work was the inclusion of convincing interpretations of the names celebrated by the mountains themselves. These by their very nature are names of antiquity and time plays havoc with spelling and pronunciation and understanding now their long-ago meaning. The 'explanations' proffered of necessity so abruptly in **The Glossary** demand a separate introductory section (the next section in the text) (an explanation, here, for each entry) (footnotes of additional explanation in similar explication in the lists themselves would have been too academic and too untidy an arrangement). So let's now leave valley (*cwm*) and lake (*llyn*) both great (*mawr*) and small (*bach*) whether blue (*glas*) or green (*glas*) or black (*du*) behind, and turn our attention (our interpretative intentions) toward the mountains (*mynyddoedd*).

The Mountains of North Wales

The 3000-foot mountains of Wales are conveniently grouped in three distinctive clusters in close company in an area of outstanding natural beauty in Gwynedd in north-west Wales. The three groups are different in character and separate in topography and terrain and are called the **Glyderau, Carneddau** and **Snowdon Hills**.

('Mountains', by the way, strictly speaking, is something of a misnomer here because these are the stumps, the partially worn-down wrecks not of mountains but of a huge *tableland*, one vast and even-domed plateau of land that once was North Wales, that the great Ice Ages and an unrelenting, remorseless, unceasing and incessantly destructive weathering has not as yet been able to completely wear away. *These* are not mountains. Mountains, subduction, mountains, volcanic eruptions, yes, *had* happened here but much much earlier, in the Ordovician Period, between 490 and 455 million years ago. All is explained in a superb new permanent bilingual exhibition which opened on 15th October 1993 at the National Museum of Wales, Cathays Park, Cardiff, called **The Evolution of Wales**. It is a very vivid multi-media journey through 4,600 million years of planetary history to tell the story of Wales from its very earliest geological origin right up to the end of the last Great Ice Age. *This* is all that's now left. It's the Ice what did it. These are not mountains.)

The scenery on the summit plateau of the **Glyderau** (tumbled heaps of massive slabs and boulders and upright shards of

42

The grey rock-ledge of **Glyder Fach** *on top of the grey-walled Cwm Bochlwyd cirque*

Glyder Fach *and its surrounding blockfield from the peak of Castell y Gwynt. The volcanic cone of rock on the left is, of course, Tryfan.*

splintered rock) make this look an eerie and an unearthly place. There are many places in the Glyderau of terrible beauty. Great amphitheatres of stark grey-walled cirques have been gouged out on north-facing flanks by glacial excavation. Here is the unequalled impression of a nakedly exposed geology. Here in the Glyderau is geological grandeur at its best.

The **Carneddau**, by way of contrast, is a vast upland grassy tract of level ground, a whale-back of a place, a high plateau of rough grassland with stony outcrops on higher ground. This is one of the largest continuous features of high ground in the British Isles. There is a marvellous all round vastness here. There are truly magnificent views of an arc of the Glyderau at the south-west corner of the Carneddau.

The **Snowdon Hills** are compacted into a massif of pronounced relief. The group is dominated by the highest and greatest mountain of them all, and their namesake, Snowdon. Mountain, precipice, cliff and lake act out their most dramatic moments hereabouts in a remarkably good imitation in winter of what could easily be mistaken for an alpine or even a Himalayan setting. This is not entirely deceptive. The Snowdon Hills, Yr Wyddfa Fawr and its kin, are the most dangerous.

Glyderau

The landscape of the Glyderau includes five summits over 3000-foot, namely:

Glyder Fawr	3279 feet	999 metres
Glyder Fach	3262 feet	994 metres
Y Garn	3104 feet	947 metres
Elidir Fawr	3030 feet	924 metres
Tryfan	3010 feet	915 metres

Glyder (plural Glyder*au*) takes derivation and meaning from the Old Welsh word *cludwair* (*cludair* (plural *cludeiriau*) is its modern equivalent), an archaic and now obsolete expression for a *Heap* or *Pile* or *Thrown in a Heap*. This is a good description of the piles of

*Castell y Gwynt, The Castle of the Wind, an outlandish outcrop
of upright shards of splintered rock and spikes and blades and blocks*

*It is an eerie and unearthly landscape alone on the rock-bestrewn plateau
near Glyder Fawr. These stones look to me like a scatter of skulls.*

massive slabs and boulders and shards of rock scattered and heaped in tumbled disarray (clutter, confusion, disorder, disarrangement) on the barren summits of the Glyderau.

Glyder Fawr and **Glyder Fach** identify two distinct tors (*torr*, olden English, meaning a heap) each with its surrounding blockfield of boulders set some distance apart on the rock-strewn platform of 'The Glyders'. This is an outlandish place. This is a stark and lunar-like landscape. This looks life-less. 'Tis a passing strange plateau on which to walk. Its impact is awesome and emotionally shocking. The Glyders' names are translated in **The Glossary** as:

Glyder Fawr *The Tumbled Disarray (of Rocks) (Rocks & Shards of Rocks) the Higher*

Glyder Fach *The Tumbled Disarray (of Rocks) (Massive Slabs & Boulders) the Lower*

Y Garn is a deceptively 'easy' name, straightforward enough it seems to translate, but original meaning and reference are difficult now to honestly define. It could mean *The Cairn* or *The Landmark* or *The Mountain* or *The Heap* or *The Rock* or *The Hoof*. *Carn*, the unmutated form of *garn*, can mean hoof and Y Garn in its shape looks *exactly* like (its appearance from most directions suggests the likeness of) an upturned hoof. There is no easy explanation. Y Garn (there are many other Y Garns in Wales) is an old name from a time long ago and its meaning (other than 'cairn') has been long forgotten.

Elidir Fawr commemorates the name of an influential North-Country Briton called *Elidir Mwynfawr* (Elidir of Great Wealth). *Elydr* is an obsolete Welsh word meaning brass or bronze (and 'brass' coincidentally is a North-of-England colloquialism for a great wealth of money). Elidir Mwynfawr married gold-haired Eurgain the Beautiful (the most beautiful girl in the world), daughter of King Maelgwn Gwynedd, the ungood Prince of Gwynedd, and so became son-in-law to this title and estate. Bronze by Gold. But Elidir was an outsider and many Welshmen felt, as they still do today, that no outsider, and certainly no Englishman, should be called the Prince of Wales and claim government over

Y Garn in the distance from Tryfan,
beyond Cwm Bochlwyd and the end of Y Gribin

Y Garn on closer inspection offers a somewhat obscene spread-eagled
appearance on my way to walk up to Cwm Clyt I mean Cwm Clyd.
Mountains, more usually, are anthropomorphised elsewhere as 'paps', but not
so prominently as this in Wales. We are not a prurient nation. There are only a
few little hills we call **bron** *or* **fron** *(q.v., q.v.).*

North Wales (*my* Prince was murdered in 1282). There was a fierce battle over the issue of Elidir's succession to gain the Welsh title of 'Prince of Gwynedd', and Elidir the Rich was killed. The local supporters of Elidir remained ever-faithful followers and erected a cairn of rocks on this high landmark of a mountain to forever keep his name. They named their memorial **Carnedd Elidir** (The Cairn of Elidir). The mountain in turn in time took his name.

There is an intriguing tale told about a lost cave and cavern in Elidir Fawr and it also concerns the lake lying cradled in an upper arm of the mountain, **Marchlyn Mawr**. Into the valley of this rock-girt lake there once came a farmer's son in search of a missing sheep. He discovered by chance the entrance to a cave. Next day he revisited the place and entered what in truth turned out to be a great and very wondrous cave. He looked in in wonder. It looked fabulous. In the centre of the cavern stood a miraculous table wrought entirely of arabesques of gold. On the table was placed a solid gold crown inlaid with a great wealth of precious gems and royal jewels all a-sparkling. The simple shepherd supposed this had once belonged to King Arthur himself (and who would ever want to contradict or correct the credulous boy). The lad reached out a hand to touch the crown but then a sudden noise burst upon his ears, an elemental and unholy din, an unbearably fearsome sound (a commotion like millions of gallons of water falling, I'll hazard a guess). He fled in terror to the entrance. Out in daylight out on the lake he beheld a coracle which carried a beautiful young maiden fair. She was pale, with pure ivory-white skin. She was slim. She was slender. She was small-breasted still. She had long locks of auburn-gold hair over her shoulder. She was more than mortal beauty. (The young shepherd was unaccustomed to attractive girls like this, you understand.) But the coracle itself was manned by a grimly-cloaked man, a boatman so dreadful, so wrathful and evil by the look of his cowl and countenance, so dread in aspect was the rower, that the youth, by now mortally terrified by the meaning of it all, fled straightway home to his father's cottage in Dinorwic (**Dinorwig**) incontinent.

Many local people used to believe in the existence of this hidden

The Pillar of Elidir and Craig Cwrwgl can be clearly seen on this face of **Elidir Fawr,** *but where on God's earth is that cave called* **Ogof y Marchlyn?**

Marchlyn Mawr *was once the scene of an apparition which enigmatically took the form of a coracle-carried pale young maiden, but the lake is now tamed of this kind of Celtic magic. Today it is a dammed reservoir.*

49

treasure, as described by the shepherd, in a cave in a cliff of Elidir Fawr. Several unsuccessful attempts were made to find it. By the shore of the lake is a hillock called **Bryn Cwrwgl** (The Hill of the Coracle) and the cliff beyond is called **Craig Cwrwgl** (The Crag of the Coracle). **Ogof y Marchlyn** (The Cave of Hidden Riches of Cwm Marchlyn Mawr) is to this day well-known by name in the neighbourhood though its actual location and adit remains elusive. It still may yet exist.

Within Elidir Fawr today there *is* a vast cavern, with an associated hydraulic system of tunnels and great turbines, which all now comprise the workings of The Dinorwic Pumped Storage Hydroelectric Station. It is the largest man-made civil engineering excavation in Europe. At night, at times of low demand on the National Grid and using off-peak electricity, the station pumps water from **Llyn Peris** (The Lake of Saint Peris) to replenish an upper lake at a high position on Elidir Fawr, in Cwm Marchlyn Mawr, yes, **Marchlyn Mawr** (The Great Stallion Lake). This lake was once enclosed by a huge natural bank of glacial moraine which has been strengthened now to develop the scheme's upper dammed reservoir. A massive amount of turbine-generated electricity can be generated almost instantly at a moment's notice by release of this stored water from the upper lake into the tunnels. These simple though massive plumbing systems are now the man-made entrails (*perfedd*) of Elidir Fawr.

(The 'purpose' of all this excavation into Elidir Fawr and the immediate generation of electrical energy is that it is a quick and cheap way to meet sudden demands imposed on the National Grid at times of high demand during the course of the day. This occurs mostly when all together in the evening we switch on electric kettles to make coffee and tea when it's time for another commercial break in the film on independent t.v.)

Elidir Fawr is best translated as *The Mountain of Elidir* and the name of its companion **Elidir Fach** then becomes *The* Hill *of Elidir* (*mawr* and *bach* here refer to relative bulk and height, the 'Greater' Elidir *Fawr* clearly the 'Mountain' and the 'Lesser' Elidir *Fach* merely its shoulder, a 'Hill').

Tryfan is a singularly imposing mountain peak isolated from all others in the Glyderau. It is geologically the remnant of what once was an Ordovician volcanic plug. It rises, ruggedly, stegasaurus-like in profile, cone-like and pyramidal from end-on, an enormous mass of bare rock. Its ridge is a backbone of boulders and, below this, three broken rib-cages of rock constitute its (costate) sides. It creates a very dramatic and indelible impact on first impression. Tryfan, most of all, reminds us that it is an exact primal likeness of what we all once used to call a mountain. It is the dark shape from a wide-awake child's imagination and nightmare at night. It is straight out of a story in a picture-book. Tryfan looks menacing from all aspects and ascents. Tryfan cannot be climbed without unease and difficulty. Tryfan cannot be ascended without firmness of foot and hold-fast of hand on rock for it is unforgivingly steep. This is the touch of bare naked rock. Here is the void of its abyss. Eleven feet less and this great mountain in the Glyderau would have registered only as a hill!

Tryfan has been translated variously as *The Three Peaks, The Three Tops, The Three-pointed Peak, The Three Stones, The Peak of the Pass, The Penetrating Peak* and *The Peak of the Passage*. In earlier accounts it has appeared as **Trifaen** and **Trevaen** (*tri* means three and *maen* means stone). An attractive though probably apocryphal explanation is that Tryfan is an amalgamation of the Welsh words *tra* and *ban*. *Tra* means extremely, exceedingly or very and *ban* means peak or lofty. *Tra-fan* (Tryfan) then has a meaning in the sense of *The Very High Peak (The Exremely-Lofty, The Exceedingly-Peaked, The Most-Peak)*. I like this interpretation, even though it may be absolutely in error, because Tryfan, however else you try to describe it, is the mountain that by its awe-striking appearance is *the* (extremely-lofty-looking) mountain (peak) in all of Snowdonia *Most Like A Mountain* (should look). I offer in **The Glossary**, for what it's worth, these three different species of meaning:

> **Tryfan**   *The Three (Buttressed) Peak*
> *The Very High Peak*
> *The Most-Like-A-Mountain Peak*

***Tryfan** is the legendary burial-place of Sir Bedwyr (Sir Bedivere).
King Arthur's semi-mythical sword Excalibur is said to lie unrusting still
on the shallow bottom of **Llyn Ogwen**, the lake over on the left.*

*King Arthur's Knights, The Brave Young Men of Eryri, are bivouacing across
the centuries in a secret cave on the left-hand side of **Y Lliwedd** patiently
awaiting the return to Cymru of This Once and Future Celtic King*

Two monoliths stand upright and close together at Tryfan's peak, at the actual location of the very summit itself. This looks most unnatural but in fact this is not an erection of mortals but a chance alignment in the work of Nature, an accidental happening during mountain-top decay (so they say). There is still a strangeness here. The Twin Stones of Tryfan are surely the stuff of Welsh Legend. But *The Remarkable Tale of Tryfan and its Two Standing Stones* had been lost from the oral tradition long ago and is unlikely now ever to be re-discovered again. The sixth-century Welshman Taliesin (the Welsh Bard whose poetic inspiration was first to be kept in manuscript), Taliesin (reborn little Gwion who had accidently drunk of the sorceress Ceridwen's cauldron and so obtained all knowledge and inspiration), Taliesin (The 'Radiant Brow' and contemporary of Merlin) tells that once upon a time there were *Three* Stones (*Tri-Faen* in the Welsh) held asunder on the summit of Tryfan.

Carneddau

The uplands of the Carneddau include seven summits over 3000-foot, namely:

Carnedd Llywelyn	3485 feet	1064 metres
Carnedd Dafydd	3423 feet	1044 metres
Pen yr Ole-wen	3211 feet	978 metres
Foel Grach	3202 feet	976 metres
Yr Elen	3152 feet	962 metres
Foel-fras	3091 feet	942 metres
Garnedd Uchaf	3038 feet	926 metres

Carneddau is the plural of the Welsh word *carnedd* which can mean *Cairn, Heap, Stack, Mound, Tumulus* or *Mountain*. Carneddau is thus a good description of this grassy upland place of whale-back mountains (tumulus-like, mound-like) with stony ground on the higher summits (heaps, scatter of stones, cairn-like stacks) and with some very ancient cairns in places.

Carnedd Llywelyn and **Carnedd Dafydd** commemorate Welsh heroes of long ago. That much is clear. The mountains for certain took their names from two Welsh Princes of the Middle Ages, but scholars are uncertain about the actual identity of the particular prince which each named mountain now immortalises.

It was at a palace (**Pen-y-bryn** perhaps) at **Aber** (**Abergwyngregyn** in full, The River-Mouth of the White Sea-Shells) on the North Wales' coast, at the base of the Carneddau mountains, that Llywelyn ap Iorwerth (Llywelyn Fawr, Llywelyn the Great, 1173-1240), one of the last (but not *the* Last) Princes of Wales, held occasional court and council (the court of the Welsh Princes was peripatetic and had no real 'home' as such here at Aber, Aberffraw, Aberystwyth, or elsewhere). Llywelyn the Great at a meeting at Aber ordered the construction of an observation post on the highest summit of the Carneddau mountains protecting him to the south. It is tempting to make fast the connection and conclude that the mountain now called **Carnedd Llywelyn** was indeed named after him and then by reasonable assumption assert that **Carnedd Dafydd** names his younger son and chosen successor, Dafydd.

This may well be so. But. But Llywelyn ap Gruffudd (ap Llywelyn) (Llywelyn ein Llyw Olaf, Llywelyn our Last Leader, 1246-1282, grandson of Llywelyn the Great), a man who figured large in Welsh History, and Dafydd ap Gruffudd, brother to Llywelyn the Last, were the two last native Welsh Princes of Wales. It is of course an historical distinction to have been the last. Llywelyn the Last was killed on a bitter and cold snowy day in the winter of 1282, on December 11th 1282, on a bridge over the River Irfon at Cilmeri near Builth (**Llanfair-ym-Muallt**) by a soldier who waited in ambush in the royal service of Edward the First of England. He was decapitated. His hacked head was sent to the English Castle at Rhuddlan (**Rhuddlan**). It was paraded through the streets of London (**Llundain**). It was stuck on a pike high up on a battlement of the Tower of London. His mutilated torso was taken by Cistercian monks and buried near Rhayader (**Rhaeadr**) at Abbey Cwm Hir (**Abaty Cwm-hir**) (The Abbey of the Long Valley). His brother Dafydd was captured early in 1283 and

Carnedd Llywelyn and Carnedd Dafydd loom behind Yr Elen

*On the great Carneddau ridge above Cwm Llafar
looking back at Carnedd Dafydd*

dragged by horses through the cobble-stone streets of Shrewsbury (**Yr Amwythig**), bleeding horribly. He was barbaricly gutted, his intestines burned before his eyes, and hanged, drawn and quartered. Parts of his corpse were distributed throughout England (**Lloegr**). The City of York (**Efrog**) received his right shoulder. King Edward the First of England, by a brilliant stroke of impudence and everlasting insult to the Welsh, appointed his own son and hier, the future Edward the Second, born at Caernarfon Castle not speaking a word of English, to be the Prince of Wales. English rule over Wales, from here on in history, was direct and absolute. It was a fatal fact. Llywelyn *was* the Last. My Prince was killed in 1282. These men, Llywelyn ap Gruffudd and his brother Dafydd ap Gruffudd, equally can claim honour of commemoration and have rightful entitlement to high elevation and immemorial remembrance in these Carneddau mountains' names. But the *other* Llywelyn's story is just as good a claim to name this as *his* eminence . . .

Llywelyn ap Iorwerth (Llywelyn the son of Iorwerth Drwyndwn, The Castle-Builder Iorwerth the Broken-Nose) was born, according to tradition, at Castell Dolwyddelan, the Welsh castle at **Dolwyddelan** (The Vale of Saint Gwyddelan), on a crag at the edge of the flood-plain of the Afon Lledr Valley under Moel Siabod (he certainly spent most of his boyhood there). Llywelyn the Great in adult life, when back at home from war and endless counsels and assembly, lived at **Trefriw** in Nant Conwy with his wife Joan (an illegitimate daughter of King John of England). It is said that the couple used to walk up into the eastern Carneddau hills to worship in the medieval church of **Llanrhychwyn** (The Enclosure of Saint Rhychwyn, a sixth century Celtic saint) (a twin-naved twelfth century church known later as 'Llywelyn's Church'). Immediately ahead, in the west, looms a vast landscape of some of the highest Carneddau hills. Carnedd Llywelyn itself can not be seen from Llanrhychwyn but Llywelyn the Great in going to church would have known Carnedd Llywelyn's position well and seen the look-out cairn (**Carnedd Llywelyn**) in his imagination.

Carnedd Llywelyn from Pen yr Helgi Du

Llywelyn, in his later years, called an important assembly of all the Welsh lords at the great Cistercian monastery of Strata Florida (**Ystrad Fflur**) (The Vale of Flowers) (The Beautiful Vale of Meadow Flowers) near **Pontrhydfendigaid** (The Bridge at the River-Crossing of the Blessing) (in Cardiganshire) (in Dyfed) (Ceredigion). He eloquently persuaded them to accept, in due course, after his death, his son Dafydd as the next ruler of Gwynedd. Llywelyn then, having gained unanimous assurance to honour and uphold in good faith his son's succession, relinquished his own kingship over the princedom of Gwynedd. Llywelyn the Great withdrew into peaceful obscurity in retirement as a monk at the great Cistercian Abbey of Aberconwy. The Abbey held land in Nant Conwy and Nant Gwynant. Llywelyn ap Iorwerth (Llywelyn the Great) died peacefully in 1240. His (inexperienced) son Dafydd, in the middle of yet another acute crisis in (impending) war in Gwynedd, died (unexpectedly) in 1246.

Carnedd Llywelyn (*The Mountain of Prince Llywelyn*) and **Carnedd Dafydd** (*The Mountain of Prince Dafydd*) (there is of course a cairn, a *carnedd*, at each summit) make famous for all time the names of two Welsh Princes of the Middle Ages. That much is clear. But which particular individuals are celebrated here we shall as likely as not now never know. History and legend are both silent on the subject. (Though I take this opportunity to decide and nominate as your man the aforesaid great spokesman for Wales Llywelyn ap Iorwerth (Llywelyn Fawr) (Llywelyn the Great) (died 1240) and, next to him, his brutally murdered grandson Dafydd (Dafydd ap Gruffudd ap Llywelyn) (The Last Welshman) (died 1283).)

Pen yr Ole-wen means something like *The Promontory (The Summit) (The Head) of the White Light (the White Slope)*. There is certainly a bright glim, a 'white light', produced on this headland when snow has fallen and the whiteness of its snow-covered summit and sides is illuminated and intensified by a day of bright sunshine. The 'White Light' (the brilliance of a snow-covered mountain top set against a deep blue winter sky) is mimicked even when ice-frost alone rimes Pen yr Ole-wen's uppermost rocks (this looks from a distance like a covering of snow but is in fact a thin and brittle veneer of ice, *verglas*, condensed from very cold air). Pen yr Ole-wen's name could also suggest the presence of a beacon at some time in its recent history. The south-eastern side of the mountain is called **Yr Ole-wen**, The White Slope.

A direct ascent of Pen yr Ole-wen, at the southernmost terminus and corner of the Carneddau, gives outstandingly good views into north-facing (ice-cut) cwms of the Glyderau.

Foel Grach each winter performs once again its repeated re-enactment of an old phenomenon, an odd periglacial effect left over from the Ice Ages. The continual freezing and thawing of

Pen yr Ole-wen is seen to best effect in afternoon light
from northern Glyderau hills

*A direct ascent of Pen yr Ole-wen's southern slope though unrelentingly
arduous nevertheless affords ever-increasing magnificent views across Nant y
Benglog to look to the skyline of The Glyders into north-facing cwms and the
surface of lakes and of course across to the great, isolated, peak of,* **Tryfan**

water upon and within the ground as the wintry frosts of winter come and go produces a patterned effect upon the ground on Foel Grach. This 'ground heave' (as it's called by the geomorphologists) subtly shifts and re-arranges larger rock fragments amongst smaller pieces and out of this slow flux of fragments is ordered a remarkable and distinctive geometry of stone-filled polygons in regular array upon the ground. The ground on Foel Grach then looks like it's pock-marked all over with an ugly excrescence of hexagonal scabs. It is a most unusual effect. This summit was given the name Foel Grach in Welsh long before the English geologists came to investigate these Carneddau uplands. **Foel Grach** in English means *The Hill-Top of Scabs*.

Foel-fras means *The Fat (Thick, Gross, Large, Rough) (Squabbish) Hill (Bare Mountain) (Top)* (yes, yes) and **Garnedd Uchaf** (recently admitted by the Ordnance Survey as the fifteenth peak of Snowdonia) (though many think this is too high an elevation and an unlikely status for so inconsequential a cairn) means *The Highest Cairn* (no, it is not) or (begrudgingly I have to admit it is) (compared with Beras Bach & Mawr and Yr Aryg, similar stacks out on the same Carneddau limb) *The Higher Heap, The Upper Stack*. Yes.

Yr Elen is almost certainly the celebration in Welsh of a personal name, *Elen* (Helen). There is a romantic story in the old legends of Wales called *The Dream of Macsen Wledig* which tells how an exceedingly beautiful Celtic Princess, Elen by name, a girl from Caernarfon, after a wondrous courtship became the wife (the dream-love) of the local Roman deputy emperor, Spanish-born (and Christian) Magnus Clemens Maximus, stationed at the nearby garrison of Segontium, a Roman known to the Celts as *Macsen Wledig* (King Macsen), the Emperor of Rome. (All this is fictional autobiography, you understand, names, places and events of undoubted historicity becoming included in a good Welsh tale from long ago and by such a transmutation it gets collected in an anthology and then enters, as if by magic, the old books of the legends and later The Mabinogion.) Elen persuaded her husband to construct for her countrymen a Roman Road running all the way

Yr Elen, a distant elegant anatomical elevation across the long plod of the intervening grassland bog of Cwm Llafar

The north-east ridge of Yr Elen (a ridge that really should be called, in Welsh, The Ridge of the Dragon's Teeth Rocks) above Cwm Caseg (already visited)

from North Wales to South Wales. Remnants of this paved *traws*-Cambria Way remain on the ground in Gwynedd, as elsewhere, as reminders of its track. It goes through the mountains from Segontium to Trawsfynydd at first. And ever afterwards the Roman Way (between one Wales and another) was called **Sarn Helen**, The Paved Road of Princess (Empress) Elen. It appears as such on Ordnance Survey Maps even to this day.

(But Sarn Helen, in truth, may be no more than a corruption of **Sarn y Lleng**, The Causeway of the Legion. Though if ever that much talked about but totally unnecessary new motorway is constructed through Wales linking North and South (from Caernarfon to Carmarthen, **Caerfyrddin** in the Welsh) then the Welsh already have a name for it. **Sarn Helen Newydd**.)

Yr Elen is a distinctive peak that would have been sighted in the distance to the south as Roman legionaries and their centurions trekked on the Roman Road to the north of the Carneddau on the final leg of the march from the Roman fort (*Caer Rhufeinig*) at **Caer Rhun** (Canovium) through the pass known as **Bwlch y Ddeufaen** (The Pass of the Two Standing Stones) along the coast from east to west to get to the garrison at Caernarfon (Segontium). The commander-in-chief of this military post had recently taken an exceptionally pretty Celtic maiden as his wife, a young local girl called Elen. This is not Welsh legend. This is Roman History.

(Segontium, an auxiliary fort, an outpost of the great regional fortress at Chester (Deva in Latin, **Caer** in Welsh) was unpopular with the soldiers. It was a bleak and spartan posting for a civilised Roman that took him to the very end of the (Roman) road in Britain. Cold, slashing rain is intrinsic and the exposed garrison looks out over a notably dull and dreary coastline. Segontium occupied the flat top of a small hill on the southeastern outskirts of (what is now) Caernarfon (**Caer-yn-Arfon**, The Fortified Town in Arfon) (**Arfon** means (The Tract of Country) Facing Toward **Môn** (Anglesey, Ongull's Island, **Ynys Môn, Mam Cymru**, The Granary of North Wales).)

(Well-educated Celts evidently considered themselves Romano-Celts (Welsh Romans) in these Roman times (The 'Welsh' of years soon to come), and freely took Latin words into their own Celtic vocabulary: *porth, pont, ffenestr, ffos, mur, aur et al* . . .)

Recent guide-books to walks in the mountains of Wales give the impression that English authors have convinced themselves that Yr Elen translates as 'The Young Deer' or 'The Hill of the Fawn'. This is absolutely unauthentic. The Welsh word *elain* meaning hind (the female of the stag) or fawn (a young deer) is too far removed from Elen (Helen) (it is easily exposed as entirely unconvincing) and we can derisively dismiss this 'derivation' as nothing less than a very amateurish kind of translation in its original (and further condemn the bilingual laziness of subsequent authors in particular for perpetuating this incompetent error elsewhere in print). Reader, do not despair. There is another more likelier etymological explanation.

Look at Yr Elen's elbow-like un-twinned peak from the High Street in Bethesda. Ask a local on the street, 'What call you that mountain that peaks up there that stands apart like an island (*eilean* in Gaelic, *ey-land* in Old Norse, anglicised to *elan, ellan*)?'. 'Her Ell-en' he'll speak it in the Welsh. Then search for the word or something similar to the sound of the spoken word in the pages of a Welsh pocket dictionary. You'll discover *elin* (*elin*, eb. ll.-au, penelin, cymal canol y fraich) meaning elbow. This just so happens to be the actual shape of the mountain. Its topography (its morphology, I mean), an unusual anatomical likeness, has a remarkable resemblance to the appearance of one's elbow when looked at in elevation. It's interesting isn't it that the word for elbow in Irish is *uillean* as in uillean pipes, the elbow-blown pipes of Ireland. This is pronounced as 'ill-un' and is closely cognate with 'ell-en' spoken by the man in Bethesda in Welsh. All is explained. Yr Elen comes from the Welsh for 'The Elbow' and the name of the mountain means *The Elbow-like Mountain*. I may, of course, be entirely wrong in all this.

Yr Elen is almost certainly the celebration of the name of Elen, a girl from the south end of Caernarfon, a local Celtic maiden, a Welsh Princess (Helen) (an anagram of your name) ('Helen' is from the Greek meaning light). 'Elen', over the centuries, has become a

63

common name for attractive young Welsh girls in this part of Gwynedd. **Yr Elen** means *The (Mountain of) (Princess) Elen (Empress Helen of The Causeway)*.

Snowdon Hills

The great massif of Snowdon Hills embraces three magnificent summits over 3000-foot, namely:

Snowdon	3559 feet	1085 metres
Garnedd Ugain	3495 feet	1065 metres
Crib Goch	3029 feet	923 metres

Snowdon has been called Snowdon (Snaudun, Snawdon) since Norman Times and its straightforward translation out of the Anglo-Saxon (*snau*, snow, and *dun*, hill) means *The Snow-Hill*.

The greatest of all Eryri's cairns once capped this great summit and in the Welsh legends it marked the burial-place of the great and legendary boulder-throwing *Rhita Gawr* (Rhita, or Rhica, the Giant), the most powerful of the Welsh giants, who killed all incoming and usurping kings and clothed himself in a cloak of their interwoven Anglo-Saxon beards, ha-ha. The great summit cairn was known to the Welsh as **Gwyddfa Rhita** (The Tomb of Rhita) or **Carnedd y Cawr** (The Cairn of the Giant) but there is no archaeological evidence whatsoever for the locally reputed burial of a giant under the cairn. The cairn was an ancient monument as far back as the Bronze Age and its position, marked by an earlier smaller cairn at its core, had evidently been established already as an original site of the greatest veneration even then. The Welsh name **Yr Wyddfa** (for the *summit* itself, not the whole mountain as we now know it) means *The Burial-Place, The Grave, The Tomb, The Tumulus, The Mound, The Monument, The Eminence, The Summit*. It was known earlier as **Yr Wyddfa Fawr** (q.v.).

This is the highest place in Wales. This is the highest place in England or Ireland. This is the most visited mountain in Britain. This is the most visited mountain in the world.

There are six classic ascents to walk to the summit of Snowdon. But you can't get away from the grampus-like sounds of the

*All the famous peaks of Snowdon (**Crib Goch, Garnedd Ugain, Snowdon**)
across the topographical gap from Glyder Fawr*

Garnedd Ugain *from the north ridge of Crib Goch
looking across Cwm Uchaf, a place that's rarely visited*

narrow-gauge rack-and-pinion little-train railway, The Snowdon Mountain Railway (**Rheilffordd Trên Bach Yr Wyddfa**), delivering unfit and invalid passengers almost to the very top (day-tripping railway passengers in summer apparel and dresses seem as absurdly out of place on Snowdon as would an anorak'd, rucsac'd alpinist look who walked fully equipped along the sun-drenched shore of Llanddwyn Bay on to Llanddwyn Island, over there in the distance, on Anglesey, with ice-axe and crampons). Except in the special condition and solitude of deep snow and bright sunlight and ice (just like that day, our first ascent together, St Hilary's Day, the coldest day of the year, January 13th, 1982, when *we* were the first mountaineers to arrive), there will otherwise always be a secret but bitterly-felt misanthropic regret on Snowdon that we can never again see this mountain quite as it was in the days of the early mountaineers. Yet. Yet despite the heavy railway traffic, mountain-bikers, other walkers, over-crowding, erosion, litter, the wearisome tramping on clinically restructured paths all the way up, despite all this impediment underfoot, arrival at the summit of Snowdon continues to offer us a soaring well-spring of inspiration and an undiminished sense of well-being and awe. The great cairn has been taken down and a concrete Ordnance Survey pillar erected instead but still, somehow, there is something (the air, the abyss, the view), that reminds us that we stand at a very sacred place that was once upon a time a great giant's grave, **Gwyddfa Rhita, Yr Wyddfa Fawr**.

Ridges radiate in many directions from Snowdon's summit in striking (even star-like) configuration (satellite photographs reveal this visually much more vividly than an unshadowed map). You must negotiate these ridges and arêtes by way of good lines of ascent from attendant hills in any adventurous attempt to climb to the top of Snowdon. Take care. Take caution. This mountain's annual toll of casualties and fatalities repeats itself with dreadful regularity. Snowdon is very deceptive. Snowdon's open invitation is a fatal attraction to walk straight into its seductive death-trap. The giant Rhita Gawr still wreaks his posthumous wrath in places like **Igam-Ogam** and **Clogwyn Coch** and **Cwm Tregalan** and with fierce anger at our intrusion takes out a bloody vengeance each year, here as elsewhere, on the ridges and rocks of this most welcoming of mountains, Snowdon. Yr Wyddfa Fawr. The Great Grave. We all should be afraid of meeting the shade of Rhita Gawr. Anglo-Saxons in particular had better beware.

Garnedd Ugain means *The Mountain (The Cairn) of (the) Twenty*. The number (20) is exact and precise but in reference to what is a question that has vexed professional scholars and amateur writers alike and leads only to evasion and obscurity. The elegant name Garnedd Ugain has long remained arcane (hidden with some kind of cabalistic meaning), but. But now. By luck. I happen to have unearthed a likely link between the mountain (the cairn) and twenty. It is my personal opinion. This is the historical hint. It is a fact that during the Roman Occupation of Britain the crack (elite) XXth (Twentieth) Legion of the Roman Army (with their headquarters at the great legionary fortress at Chester, Deva in Latin, known also as Civitas Legionum, The City of The (XXth) Legion) were stationed for a while at Segontium, that important Roman garrison outside Caernarfon we visited some pages back. The great hump-like mound of Garnedd Ugain (diminishing Snowdon to a small subsidiary triangle from this angle) (north-west-facing) surely invited a strong challenge to such determined, well-trained, disciplined, professional foot-soldiers as these (at the peak of fitness and health) to climb and conquer and call their own. It was no doubt a good observation post. The mountain was claimed by the XXth Legion as *Mons Viginti*, The Mountain of XX out of the Latin, and instruction given to local inhabitants to call it by this name. In Welsh it is **Garnedd Ugain**, *The Mountain (The Cairn) (The Hump-backed Mound) of (the) XX (The Twentieth Legion of The Roman Army)*.

Crib Goch is a spectacularly narrow ridge, an arête, with a precipice falling into an abyss on either hand. It is a gaunt edge bilaterally gouged out and ground to a sharp axe-like hone by the juggernaut movement of a great ice-cap mass separating during the last great Ice Age and retreating by slow ice-flow in opposite directions (into the Llanberis Pass and into Nant Gwynant). The resultant exposed jagged crest of Crib Goch is described as an intrusive granitic body of bed-rock which is part of the lower rhyolitic series of the Snowdon volcanic suite of Ordovician (Caradoc) age flanked by bedded pyroclastic deposits. Crib Goch of course is pure geology.

Crib Goch's many scree-slopes have a distinctly reddish (umber) hue (the north ridge in particular) and from a distance the steep-sided mountain itself takes on a reddened appearance, a darker, ruddier, shade of this its scree-tongues' tint. Crib Goch is neatly named in Welsh by combining description of the crest-like ridge with the name of the mountain's overall ruddy colour. **Crib Goch** (**Y Grib Goch**) means *The Red Ridge, The Red Arête, The Red Crest, The Red Comb, The Red Cockscomb-like (The Cristate) Ridge, The (Burnt) Umber-coloured Cristate Ridge.*

Crib Goch next to Snowdon is the most dangerous place in Britain for mountain accident and tragedy.

The Snowdon Horseshoe is the most famous ridge-walk in Wales, a classic traverse. It challenges the adventurous with a very steep scramble up the blunt-ended barrier of the east ridge of **Crib Goch** (it is the dread prospect downward that determines hasty progress upward); a precarious 'walk' along a quarter-mile crest (a scary bit of balancing on a ragged and exposed arête); a scramble up and over **The Three Pinnacles** (flank the first and second to a second draughty notch, step up the next by five or six ledges to gain, to complete the knight's move, the top of the third); a walk (still grimpen at the very edge) at the very rim of a spectacular ridge above Cwm Glaslyn on a jagged-edged crest called **Crib y Ddysgl** (The Crest of the Cup-like Concavity) rising to a shoulder to gain the trig point (the trigonometrical survey pillar) on the hump-back of **Garnedd Ugain**; an easy stroll to cross a col called **Bwlch Glas**, an isthmus at the junction of paths marked by **Maenhir**[1] (q.v.); and a final 300-foot ascent to reach the summit of **Snowdon**. Wow. The view from here, all-round, is breath-taking. Lack of humidity in the atmosphere will allow you to see, looking back, with luck, out to the west, The Wicklow Hills of Ireland ('Ireland' is The Land of Éire (Erin) (The Land of the Western Place). Go down (by

*The east peak of **Crib Goch**, from The Pyg Track, from the ground*

way of the upper section of The Watkin Path, marked by
Maenhir[(2)] (q.v.), diagonally) to **Bwlch y Saethau** (The Pass of the
Arrows) (where brave King Arthur received, when putting his
retreating enemies to flight, a mortal wound by arrow-strike).
Keep to the very edge of this ridge above Gribin where once was
placed in temporary commemoration **Carnedd Arthur** (The Once
and Future King's Cairn) (where, early last year, exactly at this
spot, I banged my right leg against a rock and unknowingly badly
hurt my knee) (my once and future knee got better, but it never
again will get altogether well). Edge carefully across to **Bwlch
Ciliau** (The Pass of King Arthur's Retreating Enemy). The

Crib Goch *from the air, looking out of the left-hand window of a circling Cessna aircraft. The east and north ridges meet at the quartz-marked east peak, there's the length of its narrow arête, and right at this end, look, The Pinnacles of Crib Goch.*

cathedral-like north-east-facing edge of **Y Lliwedd** is ascended without complication. (In a cave in a cliff-face on the left-hand side of Lliwedd, so speluncar legend has it, The Knights of The Welsh Round Table are bivouacing across the centuries. They will at once awake upon the prophesied ringing of a bell at the entrance to the cave that will signal the return of King Arthur. And so, still asleep, they patiently await a pledge of fulfilments yet to come true.) There are tremendous views from Lliwedd overlooking Llyn Llydaw and

The classic photograph of the central objectives in **The Snowdon Horseshoe**
taken from an exposed position on the jagged-edged arête
nearly half-way across Crib Goch

The crest of **Crib Goch** *and its continuation into* **Crib y Ddysgl**.
This crest is the most famous walk in Wales.
There is hardly anything to rival it even in Scotland.

Cwm Dyli. **Y Lliwedd** means *The Shade, The Swart, The Livia, The Appearance (The Aspect) of a Flood; The Sight (The View of a Flood*. The West Peak. The East Peak. **Lliwedd Bach**. Fork left and descend by rock-ledges and a stony track to grass paths toward **Cwt Falf** (The Valve-House). The lake-side of **Llyn Llydaw** (The Great Green Lake) which is crossed, near-by, by **Y Cob** (The Causeway). The Hummocks of The Horns. The Last Nail. Back to the car park at **Pen-y-pass**. There is no finer walk than this in Wales. This circuit of magnificent summits at the very edge of a great chasm of empty air, this classic traverse at the rim, this arduous six-hour walk with sustained but never too difficult scrambling, this circle, this ridge, this is, deservedly, a very famous Welsh walk. **The Snowdon Horseshoe**. There is no finer walk than this in Wales.

This, then, is an inserted explanation to further explain (without distraction and abbreviation by *in situ* footnote) the best choice of the translated meanings, given in full in **The Glossary**, of the Welsh names of the fifteen 3000-foot summits in Snowdonia, all **The Mountains of North Wales** (now explained). Now, from etymology and philology and the likes back, for a moment, to the local geography.

The Geography of The Glossary

The close-clustered grouping of mountains and attendant hills within the Glyderau, Carneddau and Snowdon Hills, the separating topography of each intervening ice-cut pass and valley, and the local geography of river and road and the Snowdonia National Park boundary marked on the map provide a convenient and natural means of cataloguing and of strictly limiting what otherwise could have easily become a spread-eagling Snowdonian geography of 'The Mountainous Areas of North Wales', a tract without border. The consequent glossary would have got out of hand and would have been unending. **The Glossary** deliberately covers only a particular part of this more general 'upland' region of North Wales because it is this selected central hinterland that most interests and attracts the high-land walker (to whom **The Glossary** in this limitation is then most usefully addressed). This 'particular part' (dividing itself very neatly into the Glyderau, Carneddau and Snowdon Hills) (the repetition of these names has got a bit monotonous), these regions, now need more precise geographical definition than that given hitherto in the text.

The **Glyderau** (that Christmas-stocking-shaped outline of mountains on the map) sweep in a unique suite of cirques and mountains from **Fronllwyd** (The Brown Breast-like Hill) to **Capel Curig** (The Chapel of Saint Curig and his mother) with river-beds and roads in the great valleys clearly defining the edge of its whole hose-like outline. Its 'sock-top', here, runs from **Pont y Ceunant** (The Bridge of the River-Gorge) near **Ty'n-y-maes** (The Farmstead-Holding of the Alluvial Meadow-land Plain) across the hills **Fronllwyd** (The Brown Breast) and **Elidir Fach** (The Hill of Elidir) to the village of **Nant Peris** (The Village of the Valley of Saint Peris).

The **Carneddau** (that roughly rectangular block of sustained upland on the map) has, for the purpose of *this* glossary, corners at **Capel Curig** (The Chapel of Saint Curig), **Pen y Castell** (The Hill of the Castle-like Rock Arrangement), **Rachub** (The Keeping) and **Pont Pen-y-benglog** (The Bridge at the End of the Valley of the Skull). Rivers and the main road (the London-Holyhead A5) in **Nant y Benglog** (The Valley of the Skull) and **Nant Ffrancon** (The Valley of the Freelance Foreigners) keep separate and divide to each side the Glyderau (on the left) and Carneddau (on the right).

The **Snowdon Hills** (that axe-head-like massif of mountains on the map) are contained by valley and road and river between **Betws Garmon** (The Chapel of Germanus the Warrior-Saint), **Beddgelert** (The Grave of Saint Celert the Hermit-Saint), **Penygwryd** (The Top of the Nantgwynant Pass at its entry into Dyffryn Mymbyr of the Fathom-wide Outstretched Arm-Reach of Sir Cai), **Nant Peris** (The Village of the Valley of Saint Peris) (the original Llanberis) and **Llanberis** (The Village of the Church of Saint Peris), and a boundary on the map drawn straight across the hills from Llanberis back to Betws Garmon. **Bwlch Llanberis** (The Pass of Llanberis) separates the Snowdon Hills from the centrally-placed Glyderau. **Nant Colwyn** (q.v.) separates the Snowdon and Eifionydd (& Hebog) Hills and **Nant Gwynant** (q.v.) keeps them (Snowdon and its satellites) apart from Moel Siabod and the Moelwyns.

This remarkable concentration of spectacularly-carved mountains in northern Snowdonia is the very essence of our perception of 'Snowdonia' itself. All else is but on the outskirts of this. This tightly-focused geography is very much closer to an older sense of meaning of the word Snowdonia and coincides closely too with its usage by hill-walkers today (Eifionydd, Moelwyni, the Arenig, Berwyn and Aran ranges, Rhinogydd and Cadair Idris Hills are all called 'outlying' hills). This, then, this central cluster of Glyderau, Carneddau and Snowdon Hills, this is the deliberately limited local geographical context chosen for compilation of **The Glossary**.

Arrangement & Interpretation of The Names

This territory of mountains has something like five hundred-odd Welsh place-names assigned a place on recent editions of (admirable) 1:50 000 (1¼ inches to 1 mile) and (excellent) 1:25 000 (2½ inches to 1 mile) Ordnance Survey Maps (**Appendix 3**). I have collected the names under each distinct mountain-range heading (**Glyderau, Carneddau** and **Snowdon Hills**), added others from other maps and readings elsewhere, arranged them all alphabetically, and thereafter attempt to interpret each its meaning in translation from the Welsh into an English explanation to finally form a glossary for mountain-walkers of seven hundred-odd (actually nearly nine hundred or thereabout by simple arithmetic count, but this includes many an alternative Ordnance Survey typography of some of the names and also some unavoidable duplication in both 'separate' but adjacent mountain-range sections because of indistinguishable overlap usually of valley-floor names and bridges and rivers at the interface each shares in common) ('seven hundred-odd' is then *in rerum natura* the more accurate count), seven hundred-odd Welsh place-names of local and topographical interest, **The Glossary**. This self-imposed challenge once in motion became irresistible, fascinating, unproductive, miscalculated, compulsive, ultimately a failure, all these things as time went on. This was a three year-long obsession until completion. This was an unexpectedly demanding undertaking.

Y Geiriadur Mawr: The Complete Welsh-English English-Welsh Dictionary compiled by H. Meurig Evans and W. O. Thomas and published by Gwasg Gomer, Llandysul, and Christopher Davies (Cyhoeddwyr) Cyf., Llandybïe (fourteenth impression 1987: first published 1958), and *Collins English Dictionary: A Dictionary of The English Language* edited by A. H. Irvine and published by William Collins Sons & Company Limited, London and Glasgow (second edition 1972: first published 1956), were the most constantly consulted of dictionaries near at hand. The University of Wales' *Dictionary of The Welsh Language*, to be shelved in the libraries like the great *Oxford English Dictionary* in thick volume-after-volume from *a* to *ywen*, is in preparation only halfway through the alphabet as yet (so *Y Geiriadur Mawr* will have to do for now).

The Welsh place-names are ordered alphabetically the way an English reader would instinctively look up a word, in the sequence of The English Alphabet:
a,b,c,d,e,f,g,h,i,j,k,l,m,n,o,p,q,r,s,t,u,v,w,x,y,z
(twenty-six letters long) which is different from The Welsh Alphabet (*Yr Wyddor*):
a,b,c,ch,d,dd,e,f,ff,g,ng,h,i,l,ll,m,n,o,p,ph,r,rh,s,t,th,u,w,y
(twenty-eight letters long), and in places this is at odds with the order in which a Welsh reader would search for a word in the Welsh. There consequently may be some confusion for bilingual

readers at first glance through **The Glossary**. I make no apology for this. **The Glossary** has been written and arranged for use by a predominently English-speaking readership (to more fully appreciate the tone and intention of the names in the Welsh). The Welsh place-names are thus listed artificially (though always strictly accurately ordered throughout) in the sequence and syntactic structure of the *English* alphabet. This, sometimes, is out of synch with the Welsh.

The definite article 'The' (and its lower-cased allomorph 'the') is added ubiquitously throughout the translations (without too indecent a violation of convention) to 'read' better in English (it would anyway have been present as a prefix in the past in the Welsh as often as not, but dropped over time in spoken and written abbreviation) (Crib Goch was **Y Grib Goch**, Cnicht was **Y Cnicht** and Cwmffynnon was **Cwm y Ffynnon**). Parentheses (usually a rebarbative barricade of brackets in a text) are here (in **The Glossary**) unobtrusively scattered throughout the English column of explanations in generous (and instructive) abundance so that such punctuation can signal to the intelligent reader an obvious omission, another synonym, an alternative interpretation, or, at worst, uncertainty in translation. The context of the brackets intuits the degree of likelihood of certainty of meaning of the enclosed vocabulary of content.

A few Welsh place-names (but in the end only a *very* few) defied my efforts to reassemble any resemblance of a likely meaning, and re-echo, uselessly, tauntingly, cryptically, their Welsh names in the 'English' column as well as the Welsh. There are then no blank spaces, you understand. This is cheating a little in places, as you may notice. A few resistant Welsh words incapable of intelligent explanation by my translation are anyway best left to one's own imagination. Let them remain there as etymological riddles. They evade my understanding.

Error in spelling or inconsistency in typographical presentation still occasionally occur for some Welsh place-names when printed out on recent editions of Ordnance Survey maps, but *chwarae teg*, fair play, these faults are now very few. Still, they urgently need authoritative correction. This is not *my* responsibility. The handful or so of 'incorrect' names, at present, have been transferred mostly intact into position in **The Glossary**.

All entries have been written and re-written at least several times over and each is a chimaera of study, concentration, alteration, agony, discovery, correction, rejection, reinstatement, approval, internal coherence, gnomic rhyme, *cynghanedd*, and, at last, established palimpsestuous pedigree (then multiply all this by nine hundred times!). This is not necessarily as difficult as it sounds because the (unexpected) fact soon emerged that out of an intimidatingly long list of unfamiliar words to translate only a (surprisingly) small number of names actually presented any real ambiguity or difficulty. Nearly all are translated very easily at first, accurately enough, direct from the Welsh into an equivalent literal meaning in English. Welsh place-names in *North* Wales have not suffered nearly so bad a history of mutilation by English misusage as that inflicted in South Wales (look what happened to **Llanilltud Fawr**, as bad an example as any in Glamorgan, for Christ's and St Illtud's sake, it's now called **Llantwit Major**) (!) and fortunately here (in North Wales) names remain (generally) uncorrupted and unchanged. This authenticity is of great assistance. The act of translation is also helped locally by an unusual kind of additional confirmation and independent check on validity. This is the recognition that a place-name is usually sufficiently self-referential in its local description of the nature and identity of the place itself (its topography, its history, its natural history, its literary association, its setting) that it can become 'recognisable' at once in any good translation. This is akin to finding the key to a cryptic crossword clue and discovering the correct answer. It is unambiguous. It indisputably 'fits'.

This commonplace kind of 'local' nomenclature has been a useful principle and field-guide throughout the work when agonising about the best interpretation of a place-name's meaning. The name in Welsh is as often as not a reflection of the place itself. Let it be known in this regard that I have visited in person or passed near by almost every one of the places entered in the lists of **The**

Glossary. In the field. Up the mountain I mean. On foot. I have ascended each mountain now many times each. One hundred and fifty-four (154) ascents to the (15) summits of Snowdonia so far in fact (**Appendix 1**). By an intricate network of many different routes ink-penned in detail on all my lined (my spiders'-webbed) maps (**Appendix 3**). I have become acquainted over the miles and over the years not only with these names on maps but with the exact nature and local identity of each named location on the ground itself. This is important. This is my main qualification and authority in attempting this particular task of translation. I know something about this territory and its terrain. I have walked it. I hope this gives some kind of reassurance to the reader.

(The complete and truly definitive study of place-names in this Welsh-speaking Welsh stronghold of Wales involves problems of translation into English the solution of which, if the task is taken not to be entirely hopeless, requires, in addition to this kind of ground-work, a good understanding and articulate knowledge of the Welsh language, acceptance and integration within the local academic community and years of local enquiry (three years, let's say, of postgraduate oral history research) into the family traditions, folk-lore and customs of the older inhabitants of these uplands (this means talking in dialect to the local Welsh hill-farmers themselves). Independently walking up mountains, nodding an acknowledgement to an occasional shepherd on a hill, learning Welsh at night-class and looking up all the Welsh words in a dictionary at his desk is only the first step (or completely the wrong direction) for a presumptuous intellectual 'outsider' to take coming in. The study inevitably would be incomplete and its glossary badly faulted in places.)

The Glossary of Welsh place-names' meanings is as exactingly accurate, as readable and as unerringly 'definitive' a list as I can render it working unassisted and alone. There was no-one around to relieve me of my ignorance. Whatever errors of translation remain remain entirely my own fault and blunder. The author unconditionally reserves the right to be wrong.

(It's all too easy in translation to make an innocent mistake. The Celtic scholar and the well-read bilingual Welshman will scoff. And besides, even if I've got things more or less right, I have no doubt that hostility and outrage will be expressed in some quarter or other and take nationalist issue with the crass stupidity of soliciting publication in English not Welsh. I'm open to criticism from all sides of Cymru you see. In this regard, with due respect, **The Glossary** is addressed to the wider readership of *English*-speaking hill-walkers and climbers, pedestrians and cragsmen alike, Welsh or not, with interest in this Welsh landscape and the language of its place-names, so they can more fully appreciate (I repeat) the tone and intention of the *Welsh*. *Croeso*, see (see page 97). Whether you like it or not, every language that comes into contact with another like this *has* to face up to and accept the requirement somewhere along the way for a good translation. **The Glossary** (I say it with just the right amount of humility) is just such a beginning. It is a bridge (a *pont*) (or rather, because it *is* faulted I'm sure in places, a *disappointed* bridge, a pier). A framework at least (for others more bilingually adept than what I am) to follow (to meticulously check over and 'correct' the legs of its rather shaky construction to take the traveller to Welsh Wales across).

I give you **The Glossary**. This, ladies and gentlemen, is it. It is completed to my own personal satisfaction. What day? Thursday. October 14th. Euston Station. Telephone box. The train is departing for Bangor. Exactly twelve years ago, Jac. To the day. That's it. **The Glossary** is finished. **The Glossary** is complete.

The several blank pages included at the back of this book make available to the reader who doubts or disagrees with a number of my interpretations of these Welsh place-names a handwritten section in which to contradict them. Correct my mistake if my translation is at fault and please, if you think of them, pencil in a more original (interpretative or apodictic) meaning. This is a good place, too, to make relevant notes and observations on your walks. You must communicate at once any matter of etymological importance by letter to the author *via* the publisher please, for the

Second Edition is already in preparation.

Now, a final word or two of sound advice.

A Note on Pronunciation

A word in your ear. Take particular care to speak these Welsh place-names by their correct pronunciation. I provide by **The Glossary** in print an understanding of the meaning of these names but cannot adequately represent them in sound. You must next learn this yourself. It's best to actually ask a Welsh-speaking person from the locality for tuition on pronunciation of local names in the Welsh. Employ the language itself in your conversation. Ask a *Cymro* (o) or *Cymraes* (o) '*Sut dach chi'n deud . . . . . . yn Gymraeg?*'. This easily spoken and uncomplicated phrase means 'How do you say . . . . . in Welsh?' and the question is pronounced (something like) 'Sit dark keen died . . . . . . un Gumwry-gh'. Repeat the answer given. *Da iawn.* It is a commonplace politeness to then say 'Thanks very much' in Welsh, '*Diolch yn fawr*'.

I'd better not venture to lead you further astray (hesitating, stumbling, stuttering into dreadful mis-pronunciations) (There is not a grammar yet published that is *An Infallible Way For A Monoglot Englishman To Pronounce Welsh Correctly*, so I here avoid the usual unintelligible confusion of a do-it-yourself-er's *Guide to Pronunciation of Words in Welsh*. I'll then not run the libellous risk of that very suspect expectation, *How To Speak Welsh In A Day*). Other than to say that the letter j, much to the embarrassment of all the Mister and Mrs Joneses in Wales, does not occur in the Welsh alphabet (it is only a recent addition in the English alphabet). And neither do k, q, z, and v (it took a long time to extract the v from Caernarvonshire). And there is no x (TA*CS*I instead of TAXI is painted in large white letters on kerbs and road-sides in some very Welsh towns so that Welsh-speaking taxi-drivers will then know e*cs*actly where to park). The Welsh letter *f* is pronounced as a v (as in of). The double-f, *ff*, is said as an eff (f) (as in off) and has the same sound as the Welsh *ph*. *c* by itself is pronounced like the see (C) in Ess Pedwar *Eck* (S4C) and on all other occasions like an English k as in the words *c*onquered *k*ingdom. *ch* is almost expectorated like the sea-aitch (ch) in the Scots word *loch* and the German word *nach*. Try saying *Foel Grach* now. 'Voil Grackh' it is. *u* is a misleading letter, spoken sometimes like an i (eye) as the English letters i and first y in *it*'s a mystery. But *du*, meaning black, is pronounced as 'dee' and double-d, *dd*, like the tea-haitch in the or that or thee. *w* in Welsh is pronounced like 'who' without the w (double-u) (*cwm* is 'koom' and not a damp valley called 'kquim'). *ll* is a voiceless l, and bears the same phonetical relation to l as th in thin does to th in this. *ll* is more easily learnt by oral (and glossal) example than I (or anyone else) can ever explain in writing (I quote, 'Place the tongue to pronounce l, closing the passage on one side of the mouth, and blow between the tongue and upper teeth on the other' or 'Try putting the tip of your tongue behind the teeth in the same position as for l, raising it so as to close the passage on one side, and breathing out', (!), which, if you try it, produces an uncanny likeness to a sort of terminal gasp, a final exhalation-from-the-death-bed kind of sound, and nothing like the Welsh double-ell *ll* hiss at all). *ll* is said something, but not much, like the English 'thl'. *ll* has no equivalent in any European language. *y* is spoken as the you I mean u you use in n*u*rse, and the Welsh words *y* and *yr* (meaning the and of the) also use this sound. It (the *y*) is *not* pronounced 'why'.

I overheard a tourist who boarded the Snowdon Sherpa bus in Caernarfon (*f* not v you see) and asked for a ticket to 'Pen Why Pass'. The next passenger's destination seemed to be somewhere called 'Penny Pass'. Both pronounced the name of the place wrong. Pen-y-pass is spoken in Welsh as 'Pen-uh-Pass', all in one breath. Later that day a couple got on a bus at Pont Bethania in Nant Gwynant and the girl clearly and insistently said 'Two-Four One-Four' (and repeated, 2-4 1-4, 2-4 1-4). It took a while before the bemused Welsh bus-driver (with assistance from several bilingual passengers) translated this to mean 'Two tickets for the village of Waun Fawr'. One-four, *Waun Fawr*! Her request when spoken in English and Welsh should have sounded and looked like 'Two Four Wine-Vowrr'. *r* is rotic.

Mispronunciation like this and other insensitivities to pronunciation are a debasement and an insult to the language. Perhaps we should not laugh too tolerantly in telling the joke later lest we ourselves (*sinn féin*) become too complacent about the many instances and insidiousnesses like this that constantly corrupt and erode away at an already fragmenting Welsh language. It would be better to mark these untutored mistakes with the contempt they deserve.

But get the pronunciation of **mynydd, ffridd** and **Capel Curig** right and Welsh-speaking locals in this Welsh cultural stronghold will quickly sense that you (the cosmopolitan outsider, the well-travelled visitor) are doing your best to understand and try. (This is especially important for the incomer who comes with the intention to settle more permanently in this part of Gwynedd. The English-speaking in-migrant. You must immediately accept on arrival that linguistic adaptation will be needed (is demanded) for integration and employment within the local Welsh community. Because if you do not (the usual arrogance, the monoglot English-speaker's conceit and hubris against using any other speech but English), you will forever remain an outsider by the sound of your Englishman's voice and an alienation will eventually embitter you to Wales. It may even make you move back to where it is you belong. Empathy with Wales and the Welsh and, especially, a very serious attempt to learn the Welsh language is what you'll need in Gwynedd.) Mountain, upland pasture and Capel Curig are pronounced in Welsh as 'munith', 'freeth' and 'Kapel Kirrig'. *s* is sibilant. *Castell* is 'Kass-teth'.

Welsh is otherwise entirely phonetic so they say. It sounds like it looks. There are no silent letters in Welsh. Every letter is pronounced. *ch, dd, ff, ng, ll, ph, rh, th* count as single sounds and all eight are individual letters within the Welsh alphabet. The stress in a Welsh word generally falls on the penultimate syllable. There is no indefinite article. If at all unsure, and I assure you you will be, I urge you to stop and ask a local shepherd '*Sut dach chi'n deud . . . . . . yn Gymraeg*?'.

Gain a much better acquaintance of all the hills and mountains you walk by saying the sound of them in the Welsh. Learn to speak them well in Welsh. Learn the right pronunciation. Here is a table to guide you:

Pronunciation of the Welsh Names of the Mountains of North Wales

mountain(s) over 3000-foot	phonetic pronunciation	an interpretation of meaning (but see the text and **The Glossary** for other kinds of explanations)
Glyderau	Gludairy (Glidairy)	The Tumbled-in-disarray Heaps
Glyder Fawr	Gludair (Glidair) Vowrr	The Disarray of Rocks the Higher
Glyder Fach	Gludair (Glidair) Varckh	The Disarray of Rocks the Lower
Y Garn	Uh Garrn	The Upturned-Hoof Cairn
Elidir Fawr	Ellid-irr Vowrr	The Mountain of Elidir the Rich
Tryfan	Truv-van	The Three-Buttressed Peak
Carneddau	Carnetheye	The Tumulus-like Mountains
Carnedd Llywelyn	Carneth Thlew-ellin	The Mountain of Prince Llywelyn
Carnedd Dafydd	Carneth Davith	The Mountain of Prince Dafydd
Pen yr Ole-wen	Pen Uhr Olla-When	The Promontory of the White Light
Foel Grach	Voil Grackh	The Hill-Top of Scabs
Yr Elen	Uhr Ell-en	The Mountain of Princess Elen
Foel-fras	Voil Vrass	The Squab Hill
Garnedd Uchaf	Garneth 'ick-'av	The Upper Stack
Snowdon Hills	Snowed-un Hills	The Snow-Hill Hills
Yr Wyddfa Fawr	Uhr Whith-var Vowrr	The Great Grave
Garnedd Ugain	Garneth Ig-gine	The Mountain of the XX
Crib Goch	Creeb Go-ckh	The Red Cristate Ridge

You will soon get going and grow in increasing confidence in pronunciation of the Welsh if from the beginning you learn to speak just a few simple phrases at first, is all, and actually then *use* these (*that*'s the trick) in the usual daily social exchanges of

83

everyday conversation. On the street. In the shop. On the bus. On a walk. Up a mountain. In bed. Thank you. Good night. Easily said expressions in Welsh like '*Sut dach chi?*' (pronounced 'Sit dark ckquay') meaning 'How are you?' (though in passing someone by, in acknowledgement, it's a common colloquialism with an empty meaning then similar to 'hiya' or 'wotcher') and:

bore da	good morning
prynhawn da	good afternoon
mae hi'n annifyr	it is awful
mae hi'n oer	it is cold
mae hi'n wlyb	it is wet
mae hi'n wyntog	it is windy
mae hi'n glir	it is clear
mae hi'n braf	it is fine
mae hi'n heulog	it is sunny
mae hi'n boeth	it is hot
bendigedig!	wonderful!
da iawn	very good
diolch yn fawr	thanks very much
mae'n ddrwg gen i	I'm sorry
dw i wedi blino	I'm tired
nos da	good night

You will quickly learn this and learn to improvise much else besides if you attend a highly recommended Welsh course called *Cwrs Wlpan* (the 'Welsh'-sounding word *wlpan* is really the Hebrew *ulpan*, and it means intensive). The programme is made available through the Extra-Mural Studies Department of the University College of North Wales (UCNW) and courses run regularly in Bangor (pronounced 'Bang-gore', *not* 'Banger'). This excellent Welsh course (*Cwrs Wlpan y Gogledd*) will give you a very good grounding indeed in conversational North Wales' Welsh.

The Glossary, then, is not *only* a check-list of explained Welsh place-names which allows the hill-walker and his companion at a glance to look up and discover the meanings of names of places and farms and fields and topographical features on the way up when out on a walk. It (this book in its entirety) (by its entertainment, erudition and encouragement) is *also* as good an introduction as any to act as an adit (an entry) into the Welsh language itself. This, perhaps, is too optimistic a claim . . .

But do remember that a language is not just a collection of words and catch-phrases, a vocabulary, a dictionary, a guide to pronunciation, commonplace remarks and platitudes like this, a glossary list, but a social medium through which the thoughts, the feelings, the culture of a united community of people with a strong cultural instinct and identity are expressed. Learn the language. Learn Welsh. Forgather with Y Cymry. (Personally speaking though, I wouldn't be seen dead at Eisteddfodau. Here is a very brittle and deep kind of Welsh that squats smug and toad-like in a tent and spits out druidic bile against the question when is a Welshman not a Welshman. It is the ugliness of a supercilious sneer that says some are more Welsh than others. This is too Welsh a Welshness for the likes of me and even, I suspect, for mad Iolo Morganwg (Edward Williams of Flemingston in the Vale of Glamorgan) (1747-1826) who, half-crazed, invented the Gorsedd of the Eisteddfod. It's peculiar, mun. Serious-faced old Welshmen in robes in high chairs on the stage doing rituals in the appointment of bards and, dancing to the sound of harps all round them, would you believe, a playful collection of scantily-dressed pubescent Welsh nymphets! Quilty. There's something very disturbing about this that's almost hum indecently pagan. And, without the right vernacular, lacking the local Welsh argot, Eisteddfodau it is in particular do make me feel an outcast and an exile in my own country, Wales.) This is *Cymru*, not Wales.

Ascents & Advice For Walkers

Good lines of ascent for the walker to reach all fifteen 3000-foot mountain-peaks within the Glyderau, Carneddau and Snowdon Hills, with a single summit as the climactic objective on each walk (to ascend each individual mountain in Snowdonia in turn one by one), are given in **Appendix 2** by naming places and landmarks and other features to aim for on the way up (and down). Other walks can be worked out for yourself by reading the guide-books and other publications chosen for inclusion in the select bibliography (**Appendix 4**) with cross-reference at all times to the relevant 1:25 000 Ordnance Survey map (**Appendix 3**). The selection of 29 ascents (**Appendix 2**) attempts to add my own ingredient of erratic originality here and there to otherwise quite familiar walks that'll take you on many an occasion by an unwaymarked way and on untrodden sheep-paths to places unfamiliar and unfrequented by most. 'Paths' have now become overcrowded and eroded track-ways to the summits (you can blame this on easy access to the great outdoors by car and the recent proliferation of unspontaneously repetitive guide-books' walks), outworn walk-ways for ramblers and families and kin that are without relief to the misanthropic walker out on his own. (But these same paths are often the best approach when out alone in the morning on an early start and, in descent, for return in the late afternoon. Otherwise, it's best to avoid them.) **Appendix 2** is a list neither for beginners nor for rambling groups like this but is addressed to the experienced hill-walker and ridge-wanderer in fitness and good health who seeks the solitary places. There are steep rock scrambles here with quite serious scrambling on certain rocks like Crib Goch and Bristly Ridge. Naturally, much is left to the walker's own imagination and inclination. Obviously, there are many important omissions. These Snowdonian uplands are vast and spacious and it would take ten years' worth of any such lists of walks to explore them well and know them all completely. **Appendix 2**, in the context of claiming familiarity with the Glyderau, Carneddau and Snowdon Hills, is only just a beginning.

The route descriptions by their design and nature do not necessarily imply a right of way. In part in places you will be trespassing on land under private ownership. This is illegal. This is trespass. (The Snowdonia 'National Park' is *not* a public park nor is it nationally-owned.) You must seek out the owner or keeper and be given his express permission to walk quickly across any such prohibited section 'without causing damage' (or else be prepared for attack on life and limb by an angered Welsh hill-farmer and his sheep-dog Mot). The National Trust has ownership or easement over vast tracts of these upland places and many of the Welsh hill-farms now. The National Trust's tactical prospectus in land and estate management asks for and secures the right of public access to the hills across what otherwise would remain a restricted area. Access is actively encouraged on land owned by the National Trust. Where exactly on the map 'trespass' begins and ends however is not always all that easy to assess on the ground (unless bluntly confronted by PRIVATE KEEP OUT notices) but common sense, a low profile and responsibility in passing through land enclosed by dry-stone walls (use a gate or style) is usually the walker's best guide in handling this rather tricky barbed-wire fence. If you are seriously concerned about trespassing with intent when planning a walk that'll take you 'off the beaten track' and want informed advice and seek landowners' permission, then it is advisable to write in the first instance (giving full description of the intended erring path of the walk that strays from the path of the right of way) to: The Snowdonia National Park Warden Service, The Snowdonia National Park Authority, Penrhyndeudraeth, Gwynedd LL48 6LS (The wonderful Welsh sound of **Penrhyndeudraeth** is pronounced as 'Pen-rhin Die-dry-th'. The name means The Promontory of The Two Strands). The Wardens keep in close communication with local hill-farmers and other landowners in this close-knit Welsh community and are at hand to advise walkers on access information and use of the countryside. They travel about in white Landrovers. Talk about access and trespass to a Park Warden in person. Avoid conflict and complaint.

(The concerns, the issues, the conservation and the interests of The Snowdonia National Park are watched over carefully by three vigilant 'custodian' groups: The Snowdonia National Park Authority already just said (a committee, in fact, of Gwynedd County Council), The Countryside Council for Wales (with its headquarters at Bangor) and The Snowdonia National Park Society (Capel Curig). The indelible impact of too many walkers out on the mountains is an urgent ecological issue of worry to all.)

These (**Appendix 2**) are fair-weather ascents. There is a great deal of 'weather' in Snowdonia (overcast skies, rain-bearing clouds, strong winds, a cold front coming in, thunderstorms, lightning, rare sunshine, lowering skies and drifting rain, driving rain, day after day of rain) (the atmosphere in Snowdonia is captured remarkably well on canvas by the local painter David Woodford and the rocks by Anthony Cain) but keep a look-out because it's all highly temperamental and can change rapidly in no time at all. The vagaries of the North Atlantic weather systems, besides embarrassing weathermen, also embarrass whole groups of weather-beaten walkers. It is precisely this inconsistency of the weather, often half-day by half-day, that constantly frustrates many a week's walk. Sky and skyline watchers get accustomed to months of mainly wet and dismal weather. Even the 'summer' has its week after week of prolonged anticyclonic gloom and every disappointed walker then gets to know full-well the meaning and feeling of, the Welsh have the exact expression for it, *hiraeth* ('a powerful nostalgic longing against which a siren's song is but a radio jingle'). Give bad days like this a miss. Await a day of 'good' weather for a much more pleasant (and far more photogenic) fair-weather ascent.

(These are fair-weather ascents. The presence of ice or snow during cold snaps in early spring, late autumn and throughout most of the winter months immediately transforms each walk into a very serious expedition indeed requiring ice-axe, crampons, winter clothing and a lot of this kind of experience and technical competence. Keep away (KEEP OFF THE MOUNTAINS IN WINTER) when it ices up and snows, unless you're physically and mentally equipped like an alpinist with expert winter-climbing skills. This (**Appendix 2**) is (then) (in winter conditions) very serious stuff indeed.)

(Unexpected earthquakes with after-shocks occur unannounced in Snowdonia surprisingly quite frequently (the latest of significance happened on July 19th 1984, July 29th 1992, October 11th 1993 and February 11th 1994), with seismic epicentres along one of

*The first mountaineer to arrive at the summit of **Snowdon** on January 13th 1982. This was our first ascent together.*

*An ascent of **Snowdon** in winter conditions is a very serious expedition indeed requiring ice-axe and crampons, technical competence, and winter-climbing skills*

several North Wales' faults, and these can measure up to 5.4 on the Richter Scale. The ground trembles. The rocks shake. Windows are broken. Chimney-pots crack and slates are displaced. There's really not a lot you can do to prepare yourself for the shock of an earthquake when it comes as you stand, a wee bit shakily at the best of times, on the brink of a suddenly rapidly vibrating Crib Goch . . .)

Clothing, equipment and other paraphernalia to take with you on walks depends on personal possessions and acquaintance with the weather. The author's own kit comprises all of the items check-listed below (invariably, without an omission) (an inventory that acts as well as a reminder to other walkers that few, if any, are inessential requirements):

worn by the walker

woollen skull-cap or cotton sun-hat
suncream on sensitive exposed parts (nose, ears, arms,
elbows, backs of hands, nape of neck)
outdoor activity shirt (Bonart) (in a breast-pocket of which is
carried a sealable pouch containing a small mirror, an Automobile
Association membership card, coins, and a £5 note), or, when
temperatures exceed 19°C throughout most of a day's walk,
a lightweight cotton (Peter England) shirt
map-holder holding a 1:25 000 Ordnance Survey map, slung
over one shoulder
loose underpants and baggy cotton trousers
(handkerchief & keys & skull-cap & sun-hat in hip-pockets)
short loop-stitch wool socks and second, outer,
pair of socks (with my trouser-bottoms tucked in)
Elastoplast plasters affixed to my heels (preventative of blisters)
a good pair of walking boots (Loveson from Dad) with good grip
on ground and rock
a neat and narrow daysac (Karrimor Hot Ice), with stabilising
hip-belt, strapped tightly but comfortably to fit securely
on my back

Do not go out into the mountains unprepared.
Take heed of the author's kit in this inventory.

carried in the daysac

survival bag
torch
overtrousers
anorak
close-fitting wool jumper
spare pair of socks

litre-container of water (or two)
first-aid basics (bandages, plasters, scissors,
etc), a toilet-paper roll, compass, a
William Buckley LMS whistle,
spare boot-laces (all this contained
in two sealable pouch-envelopes)

food (sandwiches, crisps, mixed nuts) (and a packet of salt)
summer cotton shirt and a black vest T-shirt
compact camera (but the scenery rarely transfers well onto film)
binoculars (eight times thirty magnification)
sunglasses, black beret, red neckerchief

Gloves, mitts, woollen balaclava, knee-length woollen socks, a
Chinese jacket, an elderly tweed jacket and a woollen scarf are
additional warm items of clothing worn when venturing out on the
mountains in colder conditions with any sign of the approaching
harshness and iciness of an incoming or outgoing winter. And a

thermometer is taken too (reading down to a chilling -30°C)
(attached outside to a daysac strap). Wind across snow brings
arrows of cold that can pierce all clothing.

It is vitally important to leave behind for others a well-drawn
sketch-map of the walk (in particular detail if the plan is to visit
unfrequented and pathless places) with a written description and
commentary on the intended route of the itinerary. Note down, on
this same page, the time of departure (from home) and tabulate the
estimated times of arrival (at the start-place of the walk), the length
of the walk (about how many hours it'll take you) and return (your
calculated safe return back home, o'clock). Record (succinctly) the
local weather forecast (sun, cloud, cloud-base, temperature,
temperature at 3000 feet, wind direction and speed, and changes
expected during the day) (follow all this beforehand by day-to-day
tracking of local conditions, if possible) and include any
contradictory meteorological observation as you look out the
window when you're about to set out. Add any other relevant
information. All this soon becomes routine and part of the
preparation. The evidence of this page left behind is essential (in
fact it is absolutely critical if you're out on your own) to best effect a
rescue later if you (and your party) fail to return two hours or so
later than expected.

Transport from near-by towns and villages to the foothills of the
mountains, and back, will probably be by car or bus (but local
bus-services are infrequent or non-existent in places and
time-tables, even the Snowdon Sherpa's, not always all that
convenient for walkers) (Motorists and cyclists are restricted in
having to return to a base. Bus-travellers and rail-users are
hampered in having to hang around for hours. It is an imperfect
world), or, by far the best arrangement all round, by thumbing a
lift at a good location by (beside) the side of the road. Roads are
rarely far away in Snowdonia.

Your walk should aim to find a good line of ascent (*vide*
Appendix 2). (At the beginning of a walk you could come across a
sign which reads, in Welsh, LLWYBR CYHOEDDUS. This

translates into PUBLIC (FOOT)PATH. The signpost is sometimes mistaken to mean but doesn't of course point the direction to the nearest TOILETS. Do not urinate in or defaecate near *afon, nant, ffynnon, ffos* or *llyn*.)

In the event of an accident in the hills, attract attention (call for help) by using the recognised distress signal (six whistle-blows or torchlight-flashes in quick succession) repeated after a minute's pause, and again, and again, until the signal is acknowledged (summoned help is on its way) and then continue to guide your rescuers to the accident spot. The emergency code-signal of extreme distress (SOS) (Save Our Souls) is three short three long three short blasts (audible signal) or flashes (light signal) in urgent succession repeated at one-minute intervals. If you have witnessed an accident and you are the messenger, make your way off the mountain as quickly as possible to the nearest telephone (an occupied house) (a dot and symbol 'T' on the map) (a Mountain Rescue Post & Emergency Telephone), dial (or press) 999 (this is an emergency) and ask for the Police (who then independently call out the rescue services). The Ogwen Valley Mountain Rescue Organisation or the Llanberis Mountain Rescue Team or a Royal Air Force Wessex Rescue helicopter from 'C' flight of 22 Squadron stationed at RAF Valley on Anglesey and Search and Rescue Dog Association (SARDA) teams, as required, will assemble (scramble) and quickly mobilise personnel and rescue equipment onto the mountain. Stay put. They will want first-hand information from you about the nature of the injury and the exact whereabouts of the casualty. The casualty of course, next time, could be you.

(You are about to embark into the mountains at the first opportunity. Beware. These mountains are dangerous and ruthless places to visit too casually without preparation and with inadequate protection. The terrain is treacherous, the weather malicious, and the slightest mistake (even a mere slip of a mis-placed boot) (*I* know) can end in disaster. (What are your chances of survival. I don't know. It depends on the weather. And who gets to you first. The helicopter or the carrion crow.) These are dangerous and ruthless places. The mountains are silent and indifferent to injury and pain. Do not ever venture out amongst them as an unwary

93

*Rare tranquillity by **Llyn Glas**, a quiet little lake with a two-tree'd ait*

jaunter on an uninformed excursion but take care and precaution with you at all times on any expedition into the hills. Take good heed of this last sentence of advice. Because. Because each elegant 3000-foot Snowdonian mountain in any kind of weather can cause serious injury and can kill. It happens every year. The 'trick' in such difficult places is to learn quickly, riskily, by the narrowness of a narrow escape, by unaccompanied experience out on your own, to be (otherwise) (all else being equal) absolutely safe. Solo hill-walking, especially, can be a profoundly rewarding personal experience (the solitary peripatetic hermit tradition was strong

*The author mellows out after a long day's walk by a bank of the **Afon Llafar**. **Ysgolion Duon**, The Black Ladders, in the background, await a mistake . . .*

among the Celts of the Western Margins in search, it's said, not of wild beauty but of sheer discomfort) but it demands judgement and maturity and independence of a very high order, and it carries a responsibility to make doubly sure that nothing, nothing at all, can go wrong. This is mountaineering at its best.)

There are so many great things to be seen on walks on the way up to the summits of these great mountains (awakening the senses all at once) (oak woodlands, open moorland, rugged skylines, hillsides, mountain masses, steep-sided valleys, gullies and ravines, mountain streams, cataracts of waterfalls in spate after storm, history, natural history, great lakes and little lakes, cliffs, precipices, isthmuses in between, ridges, arête, an unsteadying abyss, and panoramic long-distance all-encompassing views to take your breath away) that the walker (the wayfarer, the wanderer on foot) may tend in time to become too accustomed to these very extraordinary places (perception dulled by repetition and familiarity on too routine a trek). So. Go slowly. Go alone. Go a different and more difficult way up. Stop often. (There is rare tranquillity by the bank of a lake and beside a mountain stream.) There is exceptional beauty here. Take time to take and embrace these things.

There is the personal challenge. There is the sheer sweating physical fucking effort of it all. There is breathlessness. There is aching in leg muscles. There is agonising doubt. There is fear. There is risk (This is the magnet-attraction of all adventure). There is a moment or two of (radiant) (emotional) uplift and exhiliration (*hwyl*). There is (*je ne sais quoi*) (something else that's elusive and indescribable) (something) that slow-motion silent explosion, that state of wonder, that sense of one-ness with sun and stone, that sudden thrill of gratitude (to whom it may concern) when you reach (step into) (somewhere on the way) an entirely unexpected (some kind of) (something Nabok) (like entering by mistake the middle of the end of the rainbow) sudden situation, an unexpectedly wonderful spot! There is the final (second-wind) (now confident) push of ascent. Daring and determination conquer all difficulty. There is arrival at last at an identifiable summit. This is sublime. This is dreadful. This is a touch of vastness. This (requickening) feeling is a turbulent pleasure somewhere between admiration and fright. Do not forget or forfeit this. It will lift the natural disposition of your dampened spirit sky-high and bring you closer to happiness more than anything else, more than anything else you have ever done.

Do not allow your binoculars or collection of photographic decoys inveigle you by their deception to forget the *actuality* of these things. Do not look from a distance. Do not read second-hand accounts of others in The Great Outdoors. Get out and about. Do not procrastinate. Do not delay. *Walk* these Welsh mountains. As often as you can. For as long as you can. I advise this as a matter of great urgency. *Carpe diem* (Sieze the opportunity!), *quam minimum credula postero* (Enjoy the present day, trusting as little as possible to the future). Because later (This is for certain. This is absolutely certain). Because age (That catastrophic slide of ineluctable time. That rapid exponential decay of passion). Because incarceration (That heavy-sounding clanking-shut of the prison-cell door. This claustrophobic confinement of imprisonment). Because in. Because age, injury or incarceration some day will prevent you. You will not (you can not) escape. There's always (Atropos awaits to end our lot and all our mortal destiny) inevitably (snip!) that irreversibly sudden (that always unexpected) scythe of interruption (sooner or later) (somewhere on the way). Mercilessly. The grim cut. The discontinuity of. The Afanc of Glaslyn awakes (What's this batt about? I will this. Beside the rivering waters of, hitherandthithering walkers of. A mountain-lake is as good a place as any to. Night!). Full Stop.

Croeso

This, ladies and gentlemen, is it. I give you **The Glossary**. The primary assertion of this work (the motivation behind its composition, the purpose of its completion) is that such a list (ambitously set out to explain the meaning of seven hundred-odd Welsh place-names of local and topographical interest in the Glyderau, Carneddau and Snowdon Hills) is plainly needed (in publication in print) to fulfil the requirement for the general availability of a local source of reference (a definitive Welsh-into-English glossary) for non-Welsh-speaking hill-walkers to consult (in English) who are curious about the meanings of the alien and odd-looking place-names (entered on all local Ordnance Survey maps) encountered on all our walks in this upland territory (this circumscribed locality of northern Snowdonia) (This is the terrain they tread. This is the ground he or she is covering) and inquisitive (also) about the Welsh language too.

This book (this manuscript, this monograph, this onomatology) in its entirety (**Introduction, The Glossary, Appendices**) though written in English with one-way translation throughout *into* English is intended (ingenuously, with all honesty) to contribute in some small measure at least to a wider mutual understanding and awareness of the unique *Welsh*-ness of this distinctively mountainous and culturally very special part of the Principality of Wales. This is the fastness and kingdom of Gwynedd. This is the stronghold of Welsh-speaking Wales. You, the mountain-walker, walk into its very heart-land. This is a glossary to act as a guide. *Croeso.*

So much by way of preface. All this by way of introduction. I begin **The Glossary** as follows:

THE GLOSSARY

The Glyderau, Carneddau and Snowdon Hills:
A glossary for mountain-walkers of seven hundred-odd Welsh place-names of local and topographical interest

Glyderau	**The Glyders. The Heaps. The Piles. Thrown in Heaps. The Scatter of Stones. The Tumbled Disarray of Rocks. (The Clutter, The Confusion, The Disarrangement) (of Rocks).**
Afon Bryn Du	The Stream of the Dark Hill
Afon Bwlch-goleuni	The Stream of the Light Pass
Afon Cywion	The Stream (of the Valley) of the Animal Offspring (the Young Ones) (the Yeanlings) (the Lambs) (the Kids)
Afon Denau	The Thin Stream
	The Stream (by Glan) Dena (q.v., **Carneddau**)
Afon Dudodyn	The Stream of the Kiln-Region (Valley)
Afon Gafr	The Stream (of the Valley) of the Goat
Afon Idwal	The Stream of (Llyn) Idwal (q.v.)
Afon Las	The Grey (Blue) (Green) Stream
Afon Llugwy	The Stream of Clear Water
Afon Marchlyn-mawr	The Stream of the Great Stallion Lake
Afon Nant Peris	The River (in) the Valley of (Saint) Peris
Afon Ogwen	The River of the Rapid White (Waterfall Force) (Rhaeadr Ogwen) (q.v.)
Beudy-mawr	The Big Shippen
Blaen Cwm Cneifion	The Head (The Upper End) of the Valley of the Fleeces
Blaen-y-nant	Head-of-the-Valley
Braich y Ddeugwm	The Arm (of The Mountain) (dividing) the Two Valleys
Bronllwyd	The Brown Breast (Breast-like Hill) Fronllwydd (q.v.)
Bryn Cwrwgl	The Hill of the Coracle
Bryn Du	Dark Hill
Bryn Hwyaid	Ducks' Hill
	The Knoll of the Ducks

Bwlch Blaen Cwm Idwal	The Pass (at) The Head of Cwm Idwal (q.v.)
Bwlch Caseg-fraith	The Pass (by) (Llyn y) Caseg-fraith (q.v.)
Bwlch Dwyglydion	The Two Glyders' Pass
Bwlch Goleuni	The Light Pass
Bwlch Llanberis	The Llanberis Pass (q.v.)
Bwlch Melynwyn	The Reddish-Brown Pass
	The Auburny-Ochreous Ridge-Way
Bwlch Tryfan	The Gap of Tryfan (q.v.)
Bwlch y Brecan	The Pass of the Middle Hill
	The Pass of the Coarse Cloth Coverlet (the Counterpane Quilt) (the Blanket)
Bwlch y Cywion	The Pass (of the Valley) of the Animal Offspring (the Young Ones) (the Yeanlings) (the Lambs) (the Kids)
Bwlch y Ddwy-Glyder	The Pass (The Connection) (The Isthmus) of the Two Glyders
Bwlch y Dinas	The Pass of the Fort-like Rocks
Bwlch y Gwyddel	The Pass of the Irishman
Bwlch y Marchlyn	The Pass of the Stallion Lake
Capel Curig	The Chapel of (Saint) Curig (Saint Curig and his mother)
Carnedd Elidir	The Cairn of Elidir (Elidir Mwynfawr)
Carnedd y Fil-las	The Cairn of the Great Slaughter ('A Thousand Was Killed')
	Carnedd y Filiast (q.v.)
Carnedd y Filiast	The Cairn of the Greyhound Bitch
	Carnedd y Fil-las (q.v.)
Carnedd y Gwynt	The Cairn of the Tempest(s)
	Castell y Gwynt (q.v.)
Castell y Geifr	The Castle of the Goats
	The Imposing Natural Position of the Goats
Castell y Gwynt	The Castle of the Wind
	Carnedd y Gwynt (q.v.)

Cefn y Capel	The Ridge (The Back) (of the Village) of Capel (Curig) (q.v.)
Ceunant	River-Gorge
Clogwyn Du[1]	The Black Precipice (at the west face of Blaen Cwm Cneifion) (Clogwyn Du Ymhen y Glyder)
Clogwyn Du[2]	The Dark Cliff (at the south ledge of Cwm y Caseg-fraith)
Clogwyn Uchaf Glyder Fawr	The Upper Cliff of Glyder Fawr (q.v.)
Clogwyn y De	The Cliff of the South
Clogwyn y Geifr	The Jut (The Projection) (The Spur) of the Goats
	The Cliff of the Goats
Clogwyn y Gogledd	The Cliff of the North
Clogwyn y Grochan	The Cliff of the Cauldron
Clogwyn y Tarw	The Cliff of the Bull
	((The) Gribin Facet)
Clogwyn yr Ordd	The Arm of the Sledge-Hammer
Cneifion Duon	Black Fleeces
Craig Cwrwgl	The Crag of the Coracle
Craig Nant Peris	The Crag of the Valley of (Saint) Peris
Craig y Geifr	The Crag of the Goats
Creigiau Eryri	The Rocks of Eryri (q.v.) (Snowdonia)
	The Rocks of Eagles (Snowdonia)
Creigiau Gleision	The Grey (The Grey-Green) Crags
Creigiau'r Dena	The Rocks of the (opposite Glan) Dena (q.v., **Carneddau**)
Creigiau'r Eira	The Rocks of Snow (Snowdonia)
Creigiau'r Gelli	The Rocks of the Little Wood (The Grove)
Cwm Bochlwyd	The Grey-Sided Valley
Cwm Bual	The Valley of the Auroch
	The Valley of the Wild (European) Ox
Cwm Ceunant	The Valley of the River-Gully

Cwm Clyd	The Valley of the Sheltered (Lake)
	The Sheltered Valley
	The Cosy Cwm
Cwm Cneifio	The Shearing Valley
Cwm Cneifion	The Valley of the Fleeces
	The Valley of (the Safe Gathering of Sheep)
	(The Nameless Cwm)
Cwm-coch	The Red (scree'd) Valley
	The Red Valley (coloured 'red' with blooming heather on Yr Esgair)
	Cwm Curyll-coch (q.v.)
Cwm Curyll-coch	The Valley of the Red Falcon (the Windhover) (the Kestrel) (*Falco tinnunculus* in the ornithological texts)
	Cwm-coch (q.v.)
Cwm Cywion	The Valley of the Animal Offspring (the Young Ones) (the Yeanlings) (the Lambs) (the Kids)
Cwm Dudodyn	The Kiln-Region Valley
Cwm Gafr	The Valley of the Goat
Cwm Graianog	The Gravelly (The Boulder-bestrewn) Valley
Cwm Gwern Gof	The Valley of the Marshland of the Blacksmith('s Farm) (Gwern Gof Isaf) (q.v.)
Cwm Idwal	The Valley of (Llyn) Idwal (q.v.)
	The Valley of Idwal (the Giant)
	The Valley (of the Lake) of Idwal (Owain Gwynedd's murdered son)
Cwm Marchlyn	The Valley of the Stallion Lake
Cwm Padrig	The Valley of (Saint) Patrick (St Patrick, who may have been a Welshman anyway, was one of the first overseas' students ever to come to Britain)

Cwm Perfedd	The Valley of (Mynydd) Perfedd (q.v.)
	The Valley of the Middle (Land)
Cwm Tryfan	The Valley of Tryfan (q.v.)
Cwm y Caseg-fraith	The Valley of the Dappled-Grey (the Piebald) Mare
Cwm y Ffynnon	The Valley of the Spring (the Source and Flow of Water)
	The Valley of the Well of Water
Cwmffynnon	The Valley of the Well of Water
Dinas	The Fort (a natural fortress-like rock)
Dinas y Gromlech	The Fortress of the Cromlech
	The Fortress-like Rocks of the Cromlech-like Upright Slabs
	The Fortress of the Megaliths
	(The Columnar Cliffs)
Dinorwic	Dinorwig (q.v.)
Dinorwig	The Stronghold of the Ordovices (a British tribe living in North Wales before and during the Roman Occupation)
Drws Nodded	The Door (The Access-Way) (The Narrow Pass) (to) Protection (Safety)
Dyffryn	Valley
Dyffryn Mymbyr	The Valley of (Llynnau) Mymbyr (q.v.)
	The Valley of the (Confluences of Many Mountain Streams)
Elidir Fach	The Hill of Elidir (Elidir Mwynfawr)
Elidir Fawr	The Mountain of Elidir (Elidir Mwynfawr)
Eryri	The Abode of (Vanished) (Banished) (Snowdonian) Eagles
	The Land of (the) Snow
	The High (Mountainous) Land
	The Edge (beyond the Englishman's Pale)

Esgair Felen	The Yellow (The Yellow-Brown) Ridge (Long Ridge) (Leg)
	The Tawny Shank
Esgair y Ceunant	The Long Ridge of the River-Gorge
Ffynnon Beris	The Well of (Saint) Peris
Ffynnon Fymbyr	The Well (The Pool) of the (Confluences of Many Mountain Streams)
	Llyn Cwm-y-ffynnon (q.v.)
	Llyn Cwm y Ffynnon (q.v.)
	Llyn Cwmffynnon (q.v.)
Foel-goch	Red Hill
	Bare Red Hill (Top)
	The (Bare Hill-Top) Peak (of Cwm)-coch (q.v.)
Fron	The Breast of the Hill
	Hill-Breast
	Fron-rhedyn (q.v.)
Fron-rhedyn	Fern Hill
	Bracken Hill
	The Bracken-covered Breast-of-the-Hill
	Fron (q.v.)
Fronllwydd	The Hill of Success (Prosperity)
	The Brown Breast (Breast-like Hill)
	Bronllwyd (q.v.)
Gallt yr Ogof	The Hill (The Slope) (The Height) of the Cave
Garreg Wastad	Flat Crag
	The Level (The Flat) (Place) Rock
Gelli	The Grove (The Little Wood)
Glyder Fach	The Little Glyder
	The Tumbled Disarray (of Rocks) (Massive Slabs & Boulders) the Lower
Glyder Fawr	The Big Glyder
	The Tumbled Disarray (of Rocks) (Rocks & Shards of Rocks) the Higher

Golofn Elidir	The Column (The Pillar) of Elidir (Fawr) (q.v.)
Gorffwysfa Peris	The Resting-Place of (Saint) Peris Pen-y-pass (q.v.)
Gorphwysfa	The Resting Place (Rest & Be Thankful) The Rest House (Hotel)
Graig Du	Dark Rock
Gwaith	Works (abandoned copper ore workings)
Gwaith-maen	Stone-Works (The Battle-Stone)
Gwastadnant	The Place of Level Ground (in) the Valley
Gwern Gof Isaf	The Marshland (The Place Where Alder Trees Grow) of the Blacksmith('s Farm) the Lower
Gwern Gof Uchaf	The Marshland (The Place Where Alder Trees Grow) of the Blacksmith('s Farm) the Higher
Gwern-y-gof Isaf	Gwern Gof Isaf (q.v.)
Gwern-y-gof Uchaf	Gwern Gof Uchaf (q.v.)
Hafod Creadog	Maes Caradog (q.v.) (in 1352)
Helyg	Willows
Idwal (Cottage)	(Cwm) Idwal (q.v.) Cottage (built originally as a hunting lodge and used since 1931 as a YHA Hostel, one of the very first in fact in Britain)
Llanberis Pass	The Mountain-Pass (to and from) Llanberis (q.v., **Snowdon Hills**) Bwlch Llanberis (q.v.)
Llwybr Mwynwyr	The Miners' Path
Llwybr y Carw	The Path of the Deer (the Stag)
Llwybr y Geifr	The Path of the Goats
Llwybr yr Offeiriad	The Path of the Priest
Llwyn-bedw	The Grove of Birches
Llwyn-Peris	The Grove of (Saint) Peris

Llygad Glas	The Green Source (The Green Eye) (of Llyn Idwal)
Llyn Bochlwyd	The Lake of the Grey-Sided (Valley)
Llyn Clyd	The Sheltered Lake
Llyn Clyd Bach	The Sheltered Lake the Smaller (Pool)
Llyn Cwm-y-ffynnon	The Lake of the Valley of the Well of Water
	Ffynnon Fymbyr (q.v.)
Llyn Cwm y Ffynnon	The Lake of the Valley of the Well of Water
	Ffynnon Fymbyr (q.v.)
Llyn Cwmffynnon	The Lake of the Valley of the Well of Water
	Ffynnon Fymbyr (q.v.)
Llyn Cywion	The Lake (of The Valley) of the Animal Offspring (the Young Ones) (the Yeanlings) (the Lambs) (the Kids)
Llyn Ffrancon	Llyn Glas Mawr (q.v.)
Llyn Glas Mawr	The Great Blue Lake (a deep blue glacial lake nearly three miles in length now silted up to form a green alluvial plain, The Nant Ffrancon)
	Llyn 'Ffrancon' (q.v.)
Llyn Idwal	The Lake (of the Valley) of Idwal (the Giant)
	The Lake of Idwal (Owain Gwynedd's murdered son)
Llyn Lockwood	The Lake of (the Angler) Lockwood
	Lockwood's Lake
	Llyn Penygwryd (q.v.)
Llyn Ogwen	The Lake of the Rapid White (Waterfall Force) (Rhaeadr Ogwen) (q.v.) (an unexpectedly shallow lake with a maximum depth of but ten feet)
Llyn Penygwryd	The Lake (at) Penygwryd (q.v.)
	Llyn Lockwood (q.v.)

Llyn Peris	The Lake of (Saint) Peris
Llyn y Caseg-fraith	The Lake of the Dappled-Grey (the Piebald) Mare
Llyn y Cŵn	The Lake of the Dogs (the Hunting Hounds)
Llynnau Mymbyr	The (Twin) Lakes of (Dyffryn) Mymbyr (q.v.)
Maes Caradog	The Field (The Alluvial Plain) (The Alluvial Meadow-land) of Caractacus (the Great Celtic Leader Caradog, son of Brân ap Llŷr)
Maes Cariadog	The Field of Young Love (Attractive though this name looks and sounds, there is no such form in Welsh: it is an error of transcription of a 1768 map-drawer at the Penrhyn Estate office, perpetuated later elsewhere by mistake) Maes Caradog (q.v.)
Marchlyn Bach	The Lesser Stallion Lake The Stallion Lake the Smaller The Lesser Horse Lake
Marchlyn Mawr	The Great Stallion Lake The Stallion Lake the Greater The Great Horse Lake
Moel Berfedd	The Hill of the Middle (Ground) Y Foel Berfedd (q.v.)
Moel-y-Caseg	The Bare Hill of (Llyn y) Caseg(-fraith) (q.v.) The Bare Hill of the Mare Y Foel Goch (q.v.) (The Nameless Peak)
Mynydd Perfedd	The Mountain of the Middle (Land) The Mountain (The Hill) of Entrails
Nant Bochlwyd	The Stream (of the Lake) of the Grey-Sided (Valley)

Nant Clyd	The Stream of the Sheltered (Lake)
Nant Ddu	The Dark Stream
Nant Ffrancon	The Valley of the Freelance Foreigners
	The Valley of the Teutonic Mercenaries (the Franks)
	Nant yr Ieuanc Gŵn (q.v.)
	(The Upper Ogwen Valley)
	(The (True) Devil's Kitchen) (The Infernal Cauldron)
	(The Great Valley of a Great Glacial Lake, once-upon-a-time Llyn Ffrancon, q.v.)
Nant Gwern y Gof	The Stream of the Marshland of the Blacksmith('s Farm) (Gwern Gof Uchaf) (q.v.)
Nant Gwryd	The River of the Fathom (Width)
	Nant y Gwryd (q.v.)
Nant Peris	The Valley of (Saint) Peris
	(The village of Nant Peris) (old Llanberis)
Nant y Benglog	The Valley of the Skull
	(It is said that from Nant Conwy the peak of Tryfan resembles a human skull and is called Y Benglog, The Skull. This distant sighting at the head of Nant y Benglog may explain this valley's somewhat sinister name.)
Nant y Gors	The Stream of the Wet Ground (the Bogland) (the Morass)
Nant y Gwryd	The River of the Fathom (Width)
	Nant Gwryd (q.v.)
Nant yr Ieuanc Gŵn	The Valley of the Young Dogs
	(The phonetic forerunner of) Nant Ffrancon (q.v.)
Nant yr Ogof	The Stream (of the Hill) of the Cave
Nantygwryd	Nant y Gwryd (q.v.)

Ogof y Marchlyn	The Cave (of Hidden Riches) of (Cwm) Marchlyn (Mawr) (q.v.)
Ogwen	(The Valley of The River) Ogwen (Afon Ogwen) (q.v.)
	Ogwen (Cottage) (an old coaching inn) (owned since 1965 by The City of Birmingham Council and used now as an outdoor pursuits centre)
	(a Celtic proper name)
Pen Llyn Ogwen	The Mouth of Llyn Ogwen (q.v.)
	(Ogwen (q.v.) Cottage)
Pen y Benglog	The End (The Head) (of the Valley) of the Skull
	Y Benglog (q.v.)
Pen-y-Gwryd	Penygwryd (q.v.) (Hotel) (originally a small well-kept family ale-house, a remote wayside cottage, in the early nineteenth century, which became 'modernised' in 1847)
Pen-y-pass	The Top of the (Llanberis) Pass
	Pen-y-pass Hotel (Gorphwysfa) (q.v.)
	Gorffwysfa Peris (q.v.)
Pentre	Top Home (Farm) (The Tenant-Farmer's Place) (The Landlord's Farm-Labourer's Place)
	Homestead (Farm)
Penygwrhyd	Penygwryd (q.v.)
Penygwryd	The Head (of) (the River) (Nant) y Gwryd (q.v.)
	The Head (The Top) (The Pass) of the (Valorous) Bravery (the Manliness) (in Battle)
	The Top (of the Nantgwynant Pass at its entry into Dyffryn Mymbyr) of the Fathom (the Fathom-wide) (a Man's Length) (the Fathom-wide

	Outstretched Arm-Reach) (of Sir Cai, one of King Arthur's knights) (hence the name Penygwryd Cai, q.v.)
	Pen-y-Gwryd (q.v.)
	Penygwrhyd (q.v.)
Penygwryd Cai	Penygwryd (q.v.)
Plas y Brenin	The Manor-House (The Hall) (The Hotel) of (His Majesty) The King
	The King's Place
	(The Royal Hotel Capel Curig) (1870) (visited by Her Majesty Queen Victoria)
	(The Capel Curig Inn) (c.1800)
	(now an outdoor pursuits' centre, The National Centre for Mountain Activities, administered by The Sports' Council for England and Wales)
Pont Newydd	The New (1805) Bridge
	Pont Pen-y-benglog (q.v.)
Pont Pen-y-benglog	The Bridge (at) the End (of the Valley) of the Skull
Pont Rhyd-goch	The Bridge (at) the Red (House) River-Crossing
Pont Tal-y-llyn	The Bridge (at) the End of the Lake
Pont Tŷ-coch	The Bridge (at) the Red House
Pont Wern-gof	The Bridge (at) the Marshland of the Blacksmith('s Farm) (Gwern Gof Uchaf) (q.v.)
Pont y Ceunant	The Bridge of the River-Gorge
Pont y Gromlech	The Bridge of (Dinas y) Gromlech (q.v.)
	The Bridge of the Cromlech (the Cromlech-like Upright Slabs) (the Megaliths) (the Columnar Cliffs)
Pont y Gwryd	The Bridge of the (Nant y) Gwryd (q.v.)
Prif Glogwyn Glyder Fach	The Principal (The Main) Cliff of Glyder Fach (q.v.)
Rhaeadr Ogwen	The Rapid (The Rapidly-Flowing)

	White Waterall Force
	The Waterfall of (The River) (Afon) Ogwen (q.v.)
	The (Afon) Ogwen (and Afon Idwal) Waterfall(s) (Watersmeet)
	(Rhaeadr 'Ogwen' should more properly be called 'The Ogwen and Idwal Waterfalls' because this is where a young Afon Ogwen *and* a not much older Afon Idwal join waters to form a gigantic tumble of white water down this 200-foot bouldery glacial rock step)
Rhaeadr y Benglog	The Cataract (at the End of the Valley) of the Skull
	Rhaeadr Ogwen (q.v.)
	(The Boulder Falls)
Rhos Marchlyn	The Moor of Marchlyn (Bach & Mawr) (q.v.)
Sarn yr Afanc	The Causeway of the Water-Beast (the Beaver)
Slabiau Idwal	The Slabs (in Cwm) Idwal (q.v.)
	(Idwal Slabs)
Stablau Bont	The Stables' Bridge
Tai-newyddion	New Houses
Trigyfylchau	The Three Adjacent (Clefts)
	The (Twisting) (Turning) (Passes)
Tryfan	The Three (Buttressed) Peak
	The Three Peaks
	The Three Tops
	The Three-pointed Peak
	The Three Stones
	(The Peak of the Pass)
	(The Penetrating Peak)
	(The Peak of the Passage)
	The Very High Peak
	The Extremely-Lofty
	The Exceedingly-Peaked

	The Most-Peak
	The Most-Like-A-Mountain Peak
Tryfan Bach	Little Tryfan (q.v.)
	(Tryfan in Miniature)
Twll Du	Black Hole
	(Devil's Kitchen Cleft)
Waun Gron	Round(ed) (Gravelled) Moor
	Exposed-Place Ridge
Y Benglog	The Skull
	Pen y Benglog (q.v.)
Y Foel Berfedd	The Hill of the Middle (Ground)
	Moel Berfedd (q.v.)
Y Foel Goch	The Red Hill
	The Bare Red Hill (Top)
	Moel-y-Caseg (q.v.)
	(The Nameless Peak)
Y Galan	The Enemy
	The (Place of) (Carnage) (Massacre)
	(Mass Murder)
	The (Penis) (Penis-like) (Whetstone)
Y Gardd Madarch	The Mushroom Garden
Y Garn	The Cairn
	The Landmark
	The Mountain
	The Heap
	The Rock
	The (Upturned) Hoof
Y Gribin	The Rake-edged Ridge
Y Gwyliwr	The Sentinel
	The Watchman
Y Llymllwyd	The Grey Sharp (Severe) (Place)
Y Twll Du	The Black Hole
	(The Devil's Kitchen Cleft)
Y Waen-oer	The Cold Exposed Place
Y Waun Oer	The Cold Exposed Place
Yr Esgair	The Long (Narrow) Ridge-Shank
Yr Hafod	The Place of Summer Dwelling

Carneddau	**The Carnedds. The Cairns. The Heaps. The Stacks of Stones. The Tumulus-like Mounds. The Mountains.**
Adwyon Owen	Owen (Owain)'s Openings (Gaps) (Breaches) (Breaks)
Afon Aber	alias Afon Rhaeadr-fawr (q.v.)
Afon Bedol	The Stream of the Horseshoe Afon y Bedol (q.v.)
Afon Berthen	The Stream of the Bush
Afon Bodesi	The Stream of (the) Bodesi (q.v.)
Afon Caseg	The River of the Mare
Afon Cenllusg	The Stream of Hailstones
Afon Ddu	The Dark Stream
Afon Denau	The Thin (The Narrow) Stream The Stream (by Glan) Dena (q.v.)
Afon Dulyn	The River of the Black Lake
Afon Eigiau	The Stream (in) (Cwm) Eigiau (q.v.) The Stream (which flows to Llyn) Eigiau (q.v.)
Afon Ffrydlas	The Blue Streaming Stream
Afon Gam	The Crooked Stream
Afon Garreg-wen	The White-Rock Stream
Afon Goch	The Red Stream
Afon Llafar	The River of Utterance The Murmuring (Chattering) Stream The Re-Echoing (Resounding) Stream
Afon Llewesig	The Stream of the Little Lioness Cub
Afon Lloer	The Stream (of the Well) of the Moon
Afon Llugwy	The Stream of Clear Water
Afon Melynllyn	The Stream of the Yellow (the Yellow-Brown) Lake
Afon Ogwen	The River of the Rapid White (Waterfall Force) (Rhaeadr Ogwen) (q.v.)
Afon Porth-llwyd	The Stream of the Brown (Grey) (Holy) Entrance-Way (Port)

	The River of the Grey Portal (the Grey Gorge of Rock)
Afon Rhaeadr-bach	The Stream of the Smaller Waterfall
Afon Rhaeadr-fawr	The Stream of the Great Waterfall alias Afon Goch (q.v.)
Afon Wen	The White Stream
Afon y Bedol	The Stream of the Horseshoe Afon Bedol (q.v.)
Afon y Fron	The Stream of the Breast of the Hill
Ardincaple	Ardincaple (The Garden-in-Capel-Curig Place)
Bera Bach	The Rick (of Rocks) the Lesser The Lesser Stack The 'Lower' Stack
Bera Mawr	The Rick (of Rocks) the Greater The Great Stack The 'Higher' Stack
Bethesda	(a biblical name, a Hebrew word meaning 'House of Mercy', given to the nonconformist chapel built in 1820 and then naming the town of 'Bethesda' itself)
Bodesi	(a Celtic tribe in North Wales at the time of the Roman Occupation, and now the name of the farm-dwelling)
Bont Uchaf	The Highest Bridge
Braich Ddu	The Dark Ridge The Dark Branch (Arm) (of the Mountain) Braich du (q.v.) Braich-tu-du (q.v.)
Braich du	Braich Ddu (q.v.) Braich-tu-du (q.v.)
Braich Melyn	The Yellow (The Yellow-Brown) Arm (of the Mountain) The Tawny Arm

	Braichmelyn (q.v.)
Braich-tu-du	The Dark-Side(d) Spur (of the Mountain)
Braich-ty-du	The Ridge of the Black Farm Dwelling (House)
	Braich-tu-du (q.v.)
Braich Ty Du	The Ridge of the Black Farm Dwelling (House)
	Braich-tu-du (q.v.)
Braich y Brysgyll	The Spur of the Cudgel
Braich y Llyngwm	The Arm of the Mountain of the Valley of the Lake
Braichmelyn	Braich Melyn (q.v.)
Bron Heulog	Sunny Breast-of-the-Hill
	Sunny-Bank
Bryn Mawr	Big Hill
Bryn Poeth	Burnt (Hot) Hill
	The Sear Hill
	(The Ogwen Valley Mountain Rescue Organisation's Mountain Rescue Post)
	(and RAF helicopter landing-place)
Bryntyrch	The Hill of the Hogs (the Wild Boars)
Bwlch Cowlyd	The Pass (to Llyn) Cowlyd (q.v.)
Bwlch Cyfrwy-drum	The Isthmus of the Saddle-shaped Ridge
Bwlch Eryl Farchog	The Saddle-Pass of the Hunt-Horsemen (Y Grib) (q.v.)
Bwlch Mignog	The Boggy Pass
Bwlch-y-gaer	The Pass of the Hill Fort (the Ancient Fortified Position) (Pen-y-gaer, q.v.)
Bwlch y Gwrhyd	Bwlch y Gwryd (q.v.)
Bwlch y Gwryd	The Pass of (Fearless) Bravery (Intrepidity) (in Battle)
	Bwlch y Gwrhyd (q.v.)
Bwlch y Tri Marchog	The Pass of the Three Horsemen
Bwlch ym Mhwll-le	The Defile of the Pit-Place
Bwlch yr Hel-farchog	The Pass (The Gap) of the Gathering (Hunting) Horsemen

Bwlch yr Hela	The Way of the Gathering
	The Pass of the Hunt
Bwlch yr Ole Wen	The (High) Pass of (Pen yr) Ole-wen (q.v.)
Capel Curig	The Chapel of (Saint) Curig (Saint Curig and his mother)
Carnedd	The Cairn
	Castell (q.v.)
Carnedd Dafydd	The Cairn of Dafydd
	The Mountain of (Prince) Dafydd (Llywelyn the Great's son)
	The Mountain of (Prince) Dafydd (Llywelyn the Last's brother)
Carnedd Drystan	The Cairn of Trystan (Sir Tristram of the Arthurian Romances) (on a spur of Carnedd Llywelyn) (possibly Carnedd, q.v.)
Carnedd Fach	The Lower Cairn (on Carnedd Dafydd)
Carnedd Llywelyn	The Cairn of Llywelyn
	The Mountain of (Prince) Llywelyn (Llywelyn the Great) (Llywelyn ap Iorwerth)
	The Mountain of (Prince) Llywelyn (Llywelyn the Last) (Llywelyn ap Gruffudd)
Carnedd Pen-y-borth-goch	Carnedd Penydorth-goch (q.v.)
Carnedd Penydorth-goch	The Cairn (at) the Head of the Red Entrance-Way (Gateway)
Carreg-ar-y-rhos	Rock-upon-the-Moorland
Carreg Frân	Crow Rock
Carreg Mianog	The Mianog Rock
	Carreg Minianog (q.v.)
Carreg Minianog	The (Brinking) (Brink-edged) Rock
	The (Sharpened) (Threatening) Rock
Carreg y Gath	The Rock of the Cat
Castell	The Castle without a Name (an imposing

	natural outcrop, an innominate rock, an unnamed 'carnedd' (q.v.) at grid reference 687651)
Castell y Gwynt	The Castle-like Outcrop-of-Rock of the Wind
Cedryn	Little Cedar Trees (Farm)
Cefn Coch	Red Down (Red Hill-Ridge)
Cefn Tal-llyn Eigiau	The Long Narrow Hill (The Ridge) (at) the Forehead (the Front) (the End) of Llyn Eigiau (q.v.)
Cefn y Gwynt	The Ridge of the Wind (between Bwlch yr Ole Wen and Carnedd Fach)
Cefn yr Orsedd	The (Long) Hill of the Assembly The Hill of the Tumulus-like Hillock
Cefn Ysgolion Duon	The Back of the Black Ladders
Cerrig Cochion	Red Rocks
Ciltwllan	Corner (Hiding-Hole) Nook
Clogwyn Castell	Castle Cliff
Clogwyn Cigfran	Raven Cliff
Clogwyn Du	Dark Cliff
Clogwyn Grugog	Heathery Cliff
Clogwyn Llys	Whinberry (Bilberry) Cliff
Clogwyn Maldy	(Grinding-House) (Hone-Stone) Rock
Clogwyn Mawr[1]	Big Cliff (a spur below Crimpiau)
Clogwyn Mawr[2]	The Large Cliff (an arm to the right of the approach to Cwm Lloer from Tal y Llyn Ogwen)
Clogwyn-mawr[3]	The Great Cliff (above Capel Curig)
Clogwyn Twll Du	Black Cleft Cliff
Clogwyn y Tro	The Spur (of the Mountain) of the Turn (the Bend) The Spur (of the Mountain) of the Walk
Clogwyn yr Eryr	The Cliff of the Eagle
Clogwyn yr Heliwr	The Mountain-Spur of the Gatherer The Spur of the Huntsman
Clogwynyreryr	The Cliff of the Eagle

Cors Gwaun y Gwiail	The Bogland (The Morass) of the Moor of the Sticks (the Switch-Sticks)
Craig Braich-ty-du	The Crag of Braich-ty-du (q.v.)
Craig Braich Ty Du	The Crag of Braich Ty Du (q.v.)
Craig Cefn Coch	The Rock of the Red Hill-Ridge (the Red Down)
Craig-ddu	The Dark Crag
Craig Eigiau	The Crag of (Llyn) Eigiau (q.v.)
Craig-fawr	The Big Crag
Craig Ffynnon	The Crag of the Well
Craig Lloer	The Crag (of the Well) of the Moon
Craig Llugwy	The Crag of (Cwm) Llugwy (q.v.)
Craig Wen	The White Crag
Craig y Dulyn	The Crag of the Black Lake The Cliff-Face Precipice of Dulyn (q.v.)
Craig y Llyn	The Crag of the Lake
Craig y Tri Marchog	The Crag of the Three Horsemen
Craig yr Hysfa	The Crag of the Good Pasture Place (in the Uplands) Craig yr Ysfa (q.v.)
Craig yr Uchaf	The Crag the Highest Craig yr Ysfa (q.v.)
Craig yr Ysfa	The Crag of the Craze (the Pins and Needles Feeling, a kind of itching, the craving experienced when looking over the edge of this Horrible Height) Craig yr Uchaf (q.v.) Craig yr Hysfa (q.v.)
Craiglwyn	The Crag of the Bush (the Grove)
Creigiau Eryri	The Rocks of Eryri (q.v.) (Snowdonia) The Rocks of Eagles (Snowdonia)
Creigiau Geuallt	The Rocks of the Hollow of the Hill
Creigiau Gleision	The Grey (The Grey-Green) (The Green) Crags
Creigiau Hirion	The Lengthy (The Long) (The Tall) Rocks

Creigiau Malwod	The Crags of Slugs and Snails
	The Crags of the Terrestrial Molluscs
	The Limacine Rocks
Creigiau Rhaeadr Fawr	The Crags of the Great Waterfall (Rhaeadr-fawr) (q.v.)
Creigiau'r Eira	The Rocks of Snow (Snowdonia)
Crib y Ddannedd Draig	The Ridge of the Dragon's Teeth (Rocks) (Crib y Creigiau'r Ddannedd Draig) (the north-east ridge of Yr Elen)
Cribau	Ridges
Crimpiau	Ridges
	Edges
Cwm Bychan[1]	The Small(er) (The Little) Valley (below Drum)
Cwm Bychan[2]	The Small(er) (The Little) Valley (below Foel Grach)
Cwm Bychan[3]	The Small(er) (The Little) Valley (below Pen yr Helgi Du)
Cwm Caseg	The Valley of the Mare
Cwm Cowlyd	The (Narrow) Valley (The Ledge) (above Llyn) Cowlyd (q.v.)
	The Valley of (Llyn) Cowlyd (q.v.)
	(The Owl of Cwm Cowlyd is one of The Three Elders of The World)
Cwm Eigiau	The Valley of the Depths
	The Valley of the Flocks (the Herds)
	The Valley of (Afon) Eigiau (q.v.)
	The Valley (beyond Llyn) Eigiau (q.v.)
Cwm Llafar	The Valley of (the River) (Afon) Llafar (q.v.)
	The Valley (Full of the Sound) of Babbling (Utterance) (Re-Echoing)
	The Valley of the Sound (of re-visiting RAF helicopters)
Cwm Lloer	The Valley (of the Well) of the Moon
Cwm Llugwy	The Valley of (Ffynnon) Llugwy (q.v.)

Cwm Marwddwr	The Valley of the Stagnant (Dead) Water (the Dampness) (immediately below The Darkness of The Black Ladders)
Cwm Moch	The Valley of Pigs
Cwm Pen-llafar	The Valley of the Utmost Utterance
	The Valley of the Most Murmuring
	The Valley of the Babbling Mouth
	The Valley (at) the Mouth (the End) (the Head) (of) (Cwm) Llafar (q.v.)
Cwm Tal-y-braich	The Valley (in) Front of the Arm of the Mountain
Cwm yr Afon Goch	The Valley of the Red River
Cwmglas Bach	The Lesser Grey-Green Valley
Cwmglas Mawr	The Great Grey-Green Valley
Dol-llêch	Slab (Stone) (Rock) Meadow (Covert-Dale)
Drosgl	Rough-Ground (Place)
	Ground of Stones
Drum	The Summit
Dulyn	The (Deep) Black Lake
	The (Deep) Black Pool
Eilio	(farm cottage, now empty, below Moel Eilio)
Eryri	The Abode of (Vanished) (Banished) (Snowdonian) Eagles
	The Land of (the) Snow
	The High (Mountainous) Land
	The Edge (beyond the Englishman's Pale)
Ffos Pantyrychen	The Trench (and the Brook) of the Hollow of the Oxen
Ffos Rhufeiniaid	The Romans' Leat
	The Romans' Dyke
Ffos y Foelgraig	The Ditch (and the Brook) of the Hill of the Crag

Ffrith-y-bont	The Upland Pasture of the Bridge (Farm)
Ffrwd Cerriguniaun	Straight-Stones' Stream
Ffrwd Goch	Red Rill
Ffynnon Caseg	The Well of the Mare
Ffynnon Llocr	The Well of the Moon
Ffynnon Llugwy	The Fountain-Head of Clear Water
Ffynnon Llyffant	The Well of the Toad
	Ffynnon y Llyffaint (q.v.)
Ffynnon y Llyffaint	The Well (The Pool) of Toads
	Ffynnon Llyffant (q.v.)
Foel-fras	The Fat (Thick, Gross, Large, Rough) (Squabbish) Hill (Bare Mountain) (Top)
Foel Ganol	The Middle Hill
Foel Grach	The Hill-Top (The Bare Mountain Top) of Scabs
	The Scabbed Mountain
Foel Lwyd	The Brown (Bare) Hill (Top)
	The Holy (Grey) Bare Hill-Top
Foel Meirch	The Hill of Horses
Foelgraig	The Hill of the Crag
Gallt Cedryn	The Hill of Cedryn (q.v.)
Gallt y Mawn	The Hillside of Peat
Garnedd Uchaf	The Highest Cairn
	The Higher Heap
	The Upper Stack
Gerlan	By-the-Village
	Near-the-Church
	Beside the Brook Bank
Glan Dena	The River-bank of the (River) (Afon) Denau (q.v.)
	The River-bank of (the Sacred and Private Place) (the Ten by Ten) (a camp) (a mountaineering club's base)
Glan Llugwy	The Bank of the (River) (Afon) Llugwy (q.v.)

Gledrffordd	The Rail-Way (a flat tract of level (stone) ground, a glacial effect)
Glyn Curig	The Glen of (Capel) Curig (q.v.)
Graig Lwyd	Grey Crag
Grib Lem	The Acute Crest
	The Severe Ridge
	The Sharp Ridge
Gwaun y Garnedd	The Mountain Moorland (The Field) of Carnedd (Llywelyn) (q.v.)
	The Mountain Moorland (The Field) of the Cairn (Carnedd) (q.v.)
Gwaun-y-gwiail	The Moor of the Sticks (the Switch-Sticks)
Gwern-Saeson-fawr	The Large (The Greater) River-side Thicket & Marshland of the English
Gwernydd	Boglands
	Marshlands
Gyrn	The Cone
	Y Gurn (q.v.)
Gyrn Wigau	The Peak of the Woods
Hafod-fâch	Small Farm-Dwelling
	Farm-Dwelling (at) the Corner
Hafod-y-garreg	Farm Dwelling Place of the Rock
Hafod-y-rhiw	Farm Dwelling Place of the Slope
Hafodygors-wen	The Farm House of the Fair Bog
Helyg	Willows
Hyfrydle	The Lovely (Pleasant) Place
Llanllechid	The Church (and the Burial Place) (The Sacred Place) of (Saint) Llechid (a female saint)
Llech Ddu	The Black Slab
	The Black Rock
	The Dark Lair
Llech Lefn	Smooth (Flat) Rock
Llefn	Flat (Hill-Top)
Llethr Gwyn	The Fair (Hill-Side) Slope

Llwybr yr Offeiriad	The Path of the Priest
Llwydmor	The Large Grey (Mountain)
	(The Hill of) The Grey Sea
	(The Hill of) The Holy Ocean
Llwydmor Bach	The Small Llwydmor (q.v.)
Llwydmor Mawr	The Great Llwydmor (q.v.)
Llwytmor	Llwydmor (q.v.)
Llwytmor Bach	Llwydmor Bach (q.v.)
Llyn Cowlyd	The (Darling) Lake
	The (Bosom-Beloved) Lake
	(The Deepest Lake of North Wales)
	(Llyn Cowlyd is 259 feet deep)
Llyn Eigiau	The Lake of the (Ocean-like) Depths
	The Lake of (the Shoals of Fish)
	The Lake of (Afon) Eigiau (q.v.)
	The Lake (below Cwm) Eigiau (q.v.)
Llyn Ffrancon	Llyn Glas Mawr (q.v.)
Llyn Glas Mawr	The Great Blue Lake (a deep blue glacial lake nearly three miles in length now silted up to form a green alluvial plain, The Nant Ffrancon)
	Llyn 'Ffrancon' (q.v.)
Llyn Ogwen	The Lake of the Rapid White (Waterfall Force) (Rhaeadr Ogwen) (q.v.) (an unexpectedly shallow lake with a maximum depth of but ten feet)
Llyn y Coryn	The Lake of the Spider
	The Lake of the Tonsure (the Crown of the Head)
Maen Trichwmwd	The Stone of the Commote of (the) Three
Maeneira	Snow-Stone
Marian-mawr	The Great Shore (Gravelly Ground) (Rock Debris and Scree)
	The High Boundary
Marian Rhaeadr-fawr	The Boundary (The Cliff-Wall) of the Great Waterfall

Meini Gwynedd	The Stones of Gwynedd
Melynllyn	The Yellow (The Yellow-Brown) Lake
Moel Ddefaid	The Hill of the Sheep
	Ewes' Hill
Moel Faban	Baby Hill
Moel Wnion	Onion Hill
Mynydd Du	Dark Mountain (Territory)
	(The Tree-less Hill-Land) (The Down)
Nant Ddu	The Black Brook
Nant Fach	The Little Brook
Nant Ffrancon	The Valley of the Freelance Foreigners
	The Valley of the Teutonic Mercenaries
	(the Franks)
	Nant yr Ieuanc Gŵn (q.v.)
	(The Upper Ogwen Valley)
	(The (True) Devil's Kitchen) (The Infernal Cauldron)
	(The Great Valley of a Great Glacial Lake, once-upon-a-time Llyn Ffrancon, q.v.)
Nant Tal-y-waun	The Brook (at) the Front (the End) of the Moor
Nant Ty	Brook House
Nant y Benglog	The Valley of the Skull
Nant y Geuallt	The Brook of the Hillside-Hollow
Nant y Graig	The Brook of the Crag
Nant yr Ieuanc Gŵn	The Valley of the Young Dogs
	(The phonetic forerunner of) Nant Ffrancon (q.v.)
Ochr Fwsoglog	Mossy-Side
Ogof Rhys	The Cave (The Hiding Place) (at the head of Cwm Llafar) of Rhys Goch Eryri (a medieval Welsh Poet)
Ogwen	(The Valley of the River) Ogwen (Afon Ogwen) (q.v.)
	Ogwen (Cottage) (q.v., **Glyderau**) (a Celtic proper name)

Pant y Griafolen	The Valley of the Rowan (the Mountain Ash) Tree
Pant y Mynach	The Hollow of the Monk
Parc	Field (Enclosure) (Land) (Parc is the ultimate upland hill-farm)
Pen Cowlyd	The (End) Peak (of Creigiau Gleision, q.v.) (above) (Llyn) Cowlyd (q.v.) (at grid reference 734622, not named on any Ordnance Survey map) (Creigiau Gleision (q.v.) North Top)
Pen Helig	Pen yr Helgi Du (q.v.)
Pen Llithrig y Wrach	The Gracefully-Curved Hill of the Witch (the Sorceress) The Slippery Hill of the Hag (the Spiteful Grimalkin)
Pen Llyn Ogwen	The Mouth of Llyn Ogwen (q.v.) (Ogwen (q.v.) Cottage) (q.v., **Glyderau**)
Pen y Castell	The Hill (The Top) of the 'Castle' (the Castle-like Rock Arrangement) (the Emplacement)
Pen-y-gaer	The Hill of the (Iron Age) Hill Fort (an Ancient Stronghold) The Hill of the (rampart-and-wall and chevaux-de-frise) Fortified Position The Hill-Top of the Hill Fort (protected by Dragon's Teeth)
Pen y Waen-wen	Pen y Waun-wen (q.v.)
Pen y Waun-wen	The Edge of the White Exposed Place (the Fair Moor) Pen y Waen-wen (q.v.) Penywaun-wen (q.v.)
Pen yr Helgi Du	The Hill of the Black Hunting-Hound
Pen yr Ole Wen	Pen yr Ole-wen (q.v.)
Pen yr Ole-wen	The Promontory (The Summit) (The Head) of (The Hill of) the White Light (the Bright Beacon) (the White Slope) Pen yr Ole Wen (q.v.)

Pengarreg	The End (Head) (Top) Rock
Penygadair	The Hill of the Stronghold (Fort)
	The Hill of the Chair (the Seat of Authority)
	The Hill (Top) of the Seat (the Cradle)
Penywaun-wen	Pen y Waun-wen (q.v.)
Plas Curig	The (YHA) House (Hostel) (at) (Capel) Curig
Pont Bodesi	The Bridge of Bodesi (q.v.) Farm
Pont Gwaun-y-gwiail	The Bridge of Gwaun-y-gwiail (q.v.)
Pont Newydd	The New (1805) Bridge
	Pont Pen-y-benglog (q.v.)
Pont Pen-y-benglog	The Bridge (at) the End (of the Valley) of the Skull
Pont Rhyd-goch	The Bridge (at) the Red (House) River-Crossing
Pont Tal-y-llyn	The Bridge (at) the End of the Lake
Pont Tŷ-coch	The Bridge (at) the Red House
Pont Wern-gof	The Bridge (at) the Marshland of the Blacksmith('s Farm) (Gwern Gof Uchaf) (q.v.)
Pont y Bedol	The (single slab stone) Bridge (over) the (Afon) Bedol (q.v.)
Pont y Ceunant	The Bridge of the River-Gorge
Rachub	The Holding (The Saving)
	The Keeping (The Guarding)
Rhaeadr-bach	The Smaller Waterfall
Rhaeadr-fawr	The Great Waterfall
	The High Waterfall
	(Aber Falls)
Rhaeadr Ogwen	The Rapid (The Rapidly-Flowing) White Waterfall Force
	The Waterfall of (the River) (Afon) Ogwen (q.v.)
	The (Afon) Ogwen (and Afon Idwal) Waterfall(s) (Watersmeet)

Rhaeadr y Benglog	The Cataract (at the End of the Valley) of the Skull
	Rhaeadr Ogwen (q.v.)
	(The Boulder Falls)
Rhiwlas	The Green Hill-Incline
Rhos Bodesi	The Mountain Moor of Bodesi (q.v.) Farm
Sarn yr Afanc	The Causeway of the Water-Beast (the Beaver)
Tal-y-braich-isaf	The End of the Spur of the Mountain the Lower (Farm)
Tal-y-braich-uchaf	The End of the Spur of the Mountain the Higher (Farm)
Tal-y-llyn	The End of the Lake (Llyn Eigiau)
Tal y Llyn Ogwen	The End of Llyn Ogwen (q.v.)
Tal-y-waun	The Front of the Moor
Tan-y-bwlch	Beneath-the-Way
	Under-the-Pass
Tan-y-dderwen	Under-the-Oak
Tan-y-garth	Beneath-the-Hill
Trasbwll	(Kindred's Pit)
Twll Pant-hiriol	The Hole of the Lengthened Hollow
Tŷ Gwyn	The White House
	The White (The White-washed) (Farm Dwelling) House
Ty-slatters	The (Slatters) House
Ty'n rhôs	The Moorland Farm
Ty'n-y-maes	The Farmstead of the Field (the Alluvial Meadow-Land)
	The Holding of the (Alluvial) Plain
Tyddyn-du	The Black Farm
Tyddyn-Sabel	The (Sabel) Holding
Y Braich	The Spur (The Projecting Arm) (of the Mountain)
Y Ffos Ddyfn	The Deep Cut
Y Garth	The Hill

	The Ridge
Y Grib	The (Connecting) Ridge
	(The Link)
	Bwlch Eryl Farchog (q.v.)
Y Gurn	The Cone
	Gyrn (q.v.)
Y Lasallt	The Green Hill
	Y Lasgallt (q.v.)
Y Lasgallt	The Green Hill
	Y Lasallt (q.v.)
Y Pincin	The (pinnacle-crag at Capel Curig)
Yr Allawr Goch	The Red Altar (the furthest stone of a causeway of stones leading into Dulyn, The Black Lake)
Yr Aryg	The Aryg
	(The Long Ridge)
Yr Elen	The (Mountain of) (Princess) Elen (Empress Helen of The Causeway) (The Hill of) The Young Deer (The Hind) (The Fawn)
	The Elbow (The Elbow-like Mountain)
Yr Ole Wen	(The Hill of) The White Light
	(The Hill of) The White Slope
Ysgolion Duon	The Black Ladders (ladder-like rock-formations on the dark north face of these impregnable black cliffs)
Ysgorfeinciau	The Rampart Benches (Ledges) (grassy ledges running across the lower part of The Black Ladders)
	Ysgyfeinciau (q.v.)
Ysgyfeinciau	Ysgorfeinciau (q.v.)

Snowdon Hills	**The Hills of Snaudun, Snawdon, The Snow-Hill.**
Adwy Bwlch-du	The Gap of the Black (Crag) Pass
	The Gap of the Gloomy Pass
Adwy'r waun	The Opening of the Moor
Afon Arddu	The Stream of the Black Height (the Dark High Land)
Afon Colwyn	The River (in Nant) Colwyn (q.v.)
	The River of Colwyn (the Great Shepherd of Brân)
	The River of the (Lively) Young Dog (the Pup) (the Whelp)
	The River of (the Grove in the Valley-Bottom)
Afon Cwm Glas Bach	The Stream of the Small Green Valley
Afon Cwm Glas Mawr	The Stream of the Large Green Valley
Afon Cwm Llan	The Stream of Cwm Llan (q.v.)
Afon Gennog	The Scurfy (The Lichen-encrusted) (The Scaly) Stream
Afon Glaslyn	The River (from) Glaslyn (q.v.)
	The River of the Blue (Green) Lake
Afon Goch[1]	Red Stream
	The Stream of (Llyn) Coch (in Cwm Clogwyn)
Afon Goch[2]	Red Stream (in Cwm Tŷ-du)
Afon Gorsen	Reed Stream
Afon Gwyrfai	The River of the Winding Plain
	The River of the Crooked Tract
	The River of the (Green) Field (the Green Plain)
Afon Hwch	The Stream of the Sow
Afon Maes-gwm	The Stream of the Open-Field Valley
	The Stream of the Valley of the (Upland) Plain
Afon Merch	The Stream of the Young Maiden (the Girl) (the Young Lass)

Afon Nant Peris	The River of the Valley of (Saint) Peris
Afon Tan-yr-allt	The Stream Under-the-Hill
Afon Trawsnant	The Stream Across-the-Valley
Afon Treweunydd	The Stream of the Homestead of the Moor Lands
Afon-y-cwm	The Stream of the Valley Afon y Cwm (q.v.)
Afon y Cwm	The Stream of the Valley Afon-y-cwm (q.v.)
Allt Maenderyn	The Hill (The Height) of the (Bird) Stone The Hill (The Height) of (Fragment) (ed) Stone
Allt Moses	Moses' Hill (the biblical Moses, or Moses Griffith perhaps, Pennant's worthy servant, an untaught genius in landscape drawing who illustrated Pennant's *Tour in Wales* (1770-1773))
Beddgelert	The Grave of (Saint) Celert (Hermit-Saint Celert ap Math)
Bethania	(a biblical name given to the chapel and the hamlet and the bridge (Pont Bethania) (q.v.) in Nant Gwynant)
Betws Garmon	The Oratory (The House of Prayer) (The Chapel-of-Ease) (The Bead-House) (The Cell) of (Saint) Garmon (Warrior-Saint Germanus)
Beudy Adwy-ddrain	Cattle-House (at the) Gap of Thorns
Beudy Bedd-Owen	Cattle-House (at the) Grave of Owen (Owain)
Beudy Blaen-y-Weirglodd	Cattle-House (at the) Top of The Meadow
Beudy Cerrig-cyllau	Cattle-Building of (Pointed Stones)
Beudy Hafod-wydr	The Cattle-House of the Glass Farm Summer Dwelling House
Beudy Ty'n y ddôl	The Cattle-House of the Smallholding of the Hay-Field Meadow

Beudy Ysgubor	Cowshed Barn
Beudy'r Gelli	The Byre of the Small Wood
Beudy'r Weirglodd	The Shippen of the Meadow
Blaen y Ddol	Top of the Dale
Blaen-y-nant	Head-of-the-Valley
Braich y Foel	The Arm of the Hill
Braich-yr-arran	The Spur of (the High Place) (Yr Aran) (q.v.)
Braich-yr-oen	The Arm (of the Hill) of the Lamb (the name of a now dis-used copper mine)
Brithdir	Coarse Land
	Chequered Ground
Bron-y-fedw isaf	The Breast of the Hill of the Birch Trees (Farm) the Lower
Bron-y-fedw-uchaf	The Breast of the Hill of the Birch Trees (Farm) the Higher
Bryn Dinas	Hill of (Llyn) Dinas (q.v.)
	Hill of Shelter (Refuge)
Bryn Manllyn	Hill of the Lake-Place
Bryn Mawr	Big Hill
Bwlch Carreg y Gigfran	The Pass of the Rock of the Raven
Bwlch Ciliau	The Nook-shotten Pass
	The Pass of the Recesses (the Nooks in the Rocks)
	The Pass of the Retreats (the Hiding Places)
	The Pass of the Retreats (the Retreating Enemies of King Arthur)
Bwlch Coch	The Gap of (Crib) Goch (q.v.)
	The Red Col
	Bwlch Goch (q.v.)
Bwlch Cwm Brwynog	The Pass of the Rushy (the Place of Rushes) Valley
	The Pass of the Boggy Valley
	The Pass of the Sad Valley
Bwlch Cwm Cesig	The Pass of the Valley of the Mares
Bwlch Cwm Llan	The Pass of Cwm Llan (q.v.)

Bwlch Glas	The Green Isthmus
	The Green Col
	The Pass (above) Glas(lyn)
Bwlch Goch	The Pass of (Y Grib) Goch (q.v.)
	Bwlch Coch (q.v.)
Bwlch Gwyn	The White Pass
	The Pass of the (Ruttish) Lust
	The Pass of the Lust (a Passionate Need for a Stallion)
Bwlch Llanberis	The Llanberis Pass (q.v.)
Bwlch Maenderyn	The Pass (through) (across) (Allt) Maenderyn (q.v.)
Bwlch Maesgwm	The Pass of the Open-Field Valley
	The Pass of the Valley of the (Upland) Plain
	(Telegraph Col)
Bwlch Main	The Thin (Narrow) (Slender) Pass
	The Pass of Stones
	Bwlch-y-maen (q.v.)
	Clawdd Coch (q.v.)
Bwlch y Gwyddel	The Pass of the Irishman
Bwlch-y-maen	The Pass (The Ridge) of the Stone
	Bwlch Main (q.v.)
	Clawdd Coch (q.v.)
Bwlch y Moch	The Pass of the Pigs
	(The Gap of the Short-Cut)
Bwlch y Saethau	The Pass of the Arrows
Bwlchmwlchan	The Pass's Small Gap
	The Small Gap (The Narrowing) of the (Nantgwynant) Pass
	The Gap of the Small (Unimportant) Pass
Bwlchysaethau	Bwlch y Saethau (q.v.)
Bylchau Terfyn	Boundary Passes
Cader Ellyll	The Seat of the Goblin
	The Cradle of the Elfin Fairy
	The Stronghold of the Eldritch Fiend

Cae-newydd	New Field
Cae'r-frân	The Field of the Crow
Cae'r-gors	The Field of the Bog
Caeaugwynion	White Fields
	Fair Fields
Carnedd Arthur	Arthur's Cairn
	(The Once and Future Celtic King Arthur's Burial-Place) (Cairn)
Carnedd y Cawr	The Cairn of the Giant
Castell	Castle (an imposing natural position, a fortress-like rock, an outcrop, a 'castle')
Castell Dolbadarn	The (12th century Welsh) Castle of the Vale of (Saint) Padarn (Saint Paternus) (probably built on the instruction of Llywelyn ap Iorwerth, Llywelyn the Great)
Cefn Drum	The Long Narrow Hill of the Ridge
Cerig-y-rhŷd	Stones of the Ford
	Rocks of the River-Crossing
Ceunant Bach	The Lesser Gorge
Ceunant Llwyn-onn	(The Stream of) The River-Gully of the Little Wood (the Grove) of Ash Trees
Ceunant Mawr[1]	(The Stream of) The Large River-Gully (in Nant y Betws)
Ceunant Mawr[2]	The Great Gorge Ravine (above Llanberis)
	(The Waterfall of) The Great Ravine
Chwarel Glanrafon	Glanrafon (Glan-yr-afon, q.v.) Quarry (dis-used) (Hen Chwareli, q.v.)
Chwarenog	(Sporting (Way)) (in an ascent of Gyrn Lâs)
Clawdd Coch	The Red Embankment-Barrier
	Bwlch Main (q.v.)
	Bwlch-y-maen (q.v.)
Clogwyn	Clogwyn (Station)
	Y Clogwyn (q.v.)

Clogwyn Brith	Mottled Cliff
	Coarse Cliff
	Grey Cliff
Clogwyn Carnedd yr Wyddfa	The Precipice (of the) Cairn (of) Yr Wyddfa (q.v.)
	Clogwyn y Garnedd (q.v.)
Clogwyn Coch	Red Cliff
Clogwyn Du	Black Cliff
Clogwyn Du'r Arddu	The Dark Cliff of the Black Height (the Dark High Land)
Clogwyn Llechwedd Llo	The Cliff of (the Steep Incline) the Slope of the Calf
Clogwyn Llwyd	Grey Cliff
Clogwyn Mawr[1]	Large Cliff (a cliff on the ridge-way above Llyn Peris)
Clogwyn Mawr[2]	Large Cliff (a spur between Cwm Glas Bach and Cwm Glas Mawr)
Clogwyn Melyn	Yellow Cliff
	Tawny Cliff
Clogwyn Pen Llechen	The Cliff of the End (the Brink) (the Edge) of the (Flat) Rock (Stone) (Slab)
Clogwyn y Barcut	The Spur of the Kite (the Red Kite) (*Milvus milvus* in the ornithological annals)
Clogwyn y Bustach	The Cliff of the Bullock
Clogwyn y Ddysgl	The Jut (The Spur) (The Cliff) of (Crib y) Ddysgl (q.v.)
Clogwyn y Garnedd	The Cliff of the Cairn (of Yr Wyddfa)
	The Precipice of the (Greatest) Landmark (Yr Wyddfa Fawr)
	Clogwyn Carnedd yr Wyddfa (q.v.)
Clogwyn-y-gwin	The Crag (The Rock) (The Cliff-Rock) of Wine
Clogwyn y Person	The Cliff (The Projection) (The Nose) of the Clergyman (the Parson)
Cocyn Craflwyn	The Hillock of Craflwyn (of the Wild Garlic Grove)

135

Cocyn Perthi	The Hillock of Perthi (of the Hedges, the Bushes)
Coed Craflwyn	The Wood of Craflwyn (of the Wild Garlic Grove)
Coed Maes-llifio	The Wood of the Sawing-Field
Coed Pant-agored	The Wood of the Open Hollow (the Broad Dingle)
Coed Plas-y-nant	The Wood of Plas-y-nant (the House of the Valley)
Coed Victoria	The Wood of (Queen) Victoria
Coed-yr-allt	The Wood of the Hill (the Hillside Cliff)
Craflwyn	The Wild Garlic Grove (Hall) (Craflwyn Hall)
Craig Aderyn	Bird Crag
Craig Ddu	Black Crag
Craig Eryri	The Rock of Eagles
	The Rock of Eryri (q.v.)
	(Snowdon) (q.v.)
Craig Fach	Small Crag
Craig Gladstone	The Gladstone Rock (in which is set a slate tablet commemorating, in two languages, an oration in 1892 given by an eighty-three years' old Prime Minister, Mr W. E. Gladstone, who hereabouts addressed the People of Eryri upon a very important subject, Freedom and 'Justice to Wales'. The multitude sang Cymric Hymns and 'Land of My Fathers'. *Hen wlad fy nhadau.*)
Craig Llyn	Lake Crag
Craig Llyn Teyrn	The Crag of Llyn Teyrn (q.v.)
Craig Penlan	The Rock of the Top Bank
Craig Wen	White Crag
Craig y Llyn	The Crag of the Lake
Craig y Rhaeadr	The Crag of the Waterfall
Craig yr Adwy	The Crag of the Gap

Creigiau Eryri	The Rocks of Eryri (q.v.) (Snowdonia)
	The Rocks of Eagles (Snowdonia)
Creigiau'r Eira	The Rocks of Snow (Snowdonia)
Crib Goch	The Red Ridge
	The Red Arête
	The Red Crest
	The Red Comb
	The Red Cockscomb-like (The Cristate) Ridge
	The Burnt Umber-coloured Cristate Ridge
	Y Grib Goch (q.v.)
Crib y Ddysgl	The Ridge (The Jagged Edge) (The Crest) of the Cup (the Cup-like Concavity)
Cribau	Crests
	Ridges
	The Jagged Edges
Cwellyn	Creel Lake
	Quellyn (q.v.)
	Llyn Cwellyn (q.v.)
	Llyn Cawellyn (q.v.)
	Llyn Tardennin (q.v.)
Cwm Aelhir	The Valley of the Long Ridge (the Long Edge) (the Brow)
Cwm Beudy Mawr	The Valley of the Big Shippen
Cwm Brwynog	The Rushy (The Place of Rushes) Valley
	The Boggy Valley
	The Sad Valley
Cwm Caregog	The Stony Valley
Cwm Cesig	The Valley of the Mares
Cwm Clogwyn	The Valley of the Cliff (the Precipice)
Cwm Creigiog	The Rocky Valley
Cwm Dwythwch	The Valley of (Llyn) Dwythwch (q.v.)
	The Valley of (the Two Sow Pigs)
	The Valley of (the Two Lakes)
	Glyn Dwythwch (q.v.)

Cwm Dyli	The Valley of a Great Flow of Water (Rushing Waters) (the Deluge) (the Flood) ('Dyli' is a contraction of *dylif*)
Cwm Ffridd	The Valley of the Upland Pasture
Cwm Glas	The Green Valley
	The Grey Valley
Cwm Glas Bach	The Small Green Valley
Cwm Glas Mawr	The Large Green Valley
Cwm Glaslyn	The Valley of Glaslyn (q.v.) (Upper Cwm Dyli)
Cwm Hetiau	The Valley of the Hats
Cwm Llain	Cwm Llan (q.v.)
Cwm Llan	The Valley of (the Narrow Strip) (the Slang) (Cwm Llein) (q.v.)
	The Valley of (the Blade) (the Sword) (Cwm Llain) (q.v.)
	The Valley of (the Sacred Place) (the Church) (the Parish) (the Village) (the Hamlet of Bethania)
Cwm Llein	Cwm Llan (q.v.)
Cwm Llydaw	The Valley of (Llyn) Llydaw (q.v.)
Cwm Merch	The Valley of the Young Maiden (the Girl) (the Young Lass)
Cwm Tregalan	The Valley of the Abode of the Enemy
	The Valley of the Village of Grief
Cwm Treweunydd	The Valley of the Homestead of the Moor Lands
Cwm Tŷ-du	The Valley of the Black House
Cwm-uchaf [1]	The Higher Valley (in Cwm Tŷ-du)
Cwm Uchaf [2]	The Uppermost Valley (below Crib Goch)
Cwm y Bleiddiaid	The Valley of the Ferocious Warriors
	The Valley of the Wolves
Cwm y llan	Cwm Llan (q.v.)
Cwm yr Hafod	The Valley of the Farm House (Hafod-uchaf) (q.v.)

Cwm yr Hyrddod	The Valley of the Rams
Cwt Falf	The Valve Hut
	The Valve-House
Cytiau Gwyddelod	The Irishmen's Huts (circular stone-based 'cottages') (in Cwm Dyli)
Derlwyn	Oak-Grove
	Derwlwyn (q.v.)
Derwlwyn	Oak-Trees Wood
	Derlwyn (q.v.)
Dinas	The Fort (a hill-fort, an ancient fortified position)
Dinas Bach	The Small Fort (a natural outcrop, a fortress-like crag)
	The Fortress-like Rocks the Smaller (near Dinas Mot, q.v.)
Dinas Emrys	The Fortress of Emrys (Ambrosius, called Emrys by the Welsh, brother of Uther Pendragon, the father of King Arthur himself)
	The Fortress of Emrys (Myrddin Emrys) (Merlin) (a legendary medieval Welsh magician)
	Merlin's Fort
	Merlin the Magician's Impregnable Position
Dinas-moch	The (Early) Position
	(The Quick Way to Dinas, q.v.)
	(The Refuge of Pigs) (The Pigs' Place of Shelter)
Dinas Mot	(The Defensive Position) (The Cliff-Face) Fort Mot
	The Fortress of Mot ('Mot' is a name commonly given by local shepherds to a good and obedient sheep-dog, the Welsh Border Collie)
Dinas Tŷ-du	The (Iron Age) Hill-Fort of the Black House (Farm)

Dorlan Ddu	The Dark Undercut (River) Bank
Eryri	The Abode of (Vanished) (Banished) (Snowdonian) Eagles
	The Land of (the) Snow
	The High (Mountainous) Land
	The Edge (beyond the Englishman's Pale)
Ffos y Gelli	The Ditch (and the Brook) of the Small Wood
Ffridd-isaf	The Upland Pasture (Farm) the Lower
Ffridd Uchaf	The Upland Pasture (Farm) the Higher
Ficerdy	The Vicar's House (The Vicarage)
Foel Goch	Red Hill
	The Bare Red Hill (Top)
Foel Gron	Round Hill
	The Bare Round Hill (Top)
Gallt y Llyn	The (Wooded) Hill of the Lake
Gallt y Wenallt	The Hill (The Height) of the White (Holy) (Hallowed) (Revered) (Fair) Wooded Hillside (Slope) (Y Wenallt) (q.v.)
Garnedd Ugain	The Mountain (The Cairn) of (the) Twenty (20)
	The Mountain (The Hump-backed Mound) of (the) XX (the Twentieth Legion of the Roman Army)
	The Cairn (of Wgan)
	Garnedd Ungain (q.v.)
Garnedd Ungain	The Cairn of the Elegant-One
	Garnedd Ugain (q.v.)
Geirth	Geirth
	(Enclosures)
	(The Garth)
Glan Llyn	The Shore of the Lake
Glan-yr-afon	Bank-of-the-River
Glanaber	The Bank (at) the Confluence of Rivers

Glaslyn	The Blue (Green) Lake
	Llyn Glaslyn (q.v.)
	Llyn Ffynnon Las (q.v.)
	Llyn y Ffynnon Las (q.v.)
Glyn Dwythwch	The Valley of (Llyn) Dwythwch (q.v.)
	Cwm Dwythwch (q.v.)
Goleugoed	The Light (The Open Space) (The Aperture) (in) the Wood
	(one of only two places from where to see a white horse) (through) Light (an opening, an aperture) (in the dense forest cover of the Nant Gwynant) Wood
Gorffwysfa Peris	The Resting-Place of (Saint) Peris
	Pen-y-pass (q.v.)
Gorphwysfa	The Resting Place (Rest & Be Thankful)
	The Rest House (Hotel)
Gorsaf y Copa	Station of the Summit (Summit Station)
Gribin	The (Snowdon) Gribin
	The (Short) (The Short-Cut) Ridge (from the outflow of Glaslyn up to Bwlch y Saethau and thence, on the east edge, to the summit of Snowdon)
Gwastadannas	Gwastad (Level-Place) (The Plain) annas
	The Valley-Floor Plain of (the Deer)
Gwastadnant	The Place of Level Ground (in) the Valley
Gwernlas-deg	The Fine Green Alder Trees Place
	Wernlas-deg (q.v.)
Gwyddfa Rhita	The Grave of Rhita (the Giant)
	(Snowdon's Summit Cairn)
Gyrn Lâs	The Grey-Green Peak
	The Grey-Green Stack
	The Grey-Green Horn
Hafod Llydan	The Wide Farm House (a place of summer dwelling)
Hafod Rhisgl	Bark Farm

Hafod-uchaf	The Highest Upland Farm House (Summer Dwelling)
Hafod-wydr	The Glass Farm Summer Dwelling House
Hafod-y-llan	The Farm House of (the Narrow Strip) (the Slang) (the Blade) (the Sword) (the Sacred Place) (the Church) (the Parish) (the Village) (the Hamlet of Bethania)
Hafod-y-porth	The Farm House of the Entrance-Way (the Landing Place)
Hafodty	The Farm House (The Place of Summer Dwelling)
Hafodty Newydd	The New Farm House (The New Place of Summer Dwelling)
Hanner y Ffordd	Half the Way (Up) (Station) Half the Distance (Half-Way Station) Halfway (House) (Station)
Hebron	Hebron (Station) (a biblical name, taken from an old nonconformist chapel near-by the railway line)
Helfa	The Gathering The Hunt (The Hunting Ground)
Helfa Aelgerth	The Gathering (The Hunt) (The Hunting Ground) of (Yr) Aelgerth (q.v.)
Helfa-fain	The Small Gathering (The Slim Catch) The Small Hunt (The Small Hunting Ground)
Helfa-fawr	The Great Gathering (The Big Catch) The Great Hunt (The Great Hunting Ground)
Hen Chwareli	(Dis-used) Old Quarries (Mines and Pits) (*passim*)
Igam-Ogam	The Zig-Zag
Llam-y-trwsgl	The Leap (The Jump) (The Fate) of the Clumsy

Llan-y-trwsgl	(an Ordnance Survey typographical error which should read Llam-y-trwsgl, q.v.)
Llanberis	(The village of) The Church of (Saint) Peris
Llanberis Pass	The Mountain-Pass (to and from) Llanberis (q.v.)
	Bwlch Llanberis (q.v.)
Llechog[1]	Rocky (Stony) (Slaby) (Place) (Cwm Glas Bach)
Llechog[2]	Rocky (Stony) (Slaby) (Place) (Cwm Clogwyn)
Lliwedd Bach	The Smaller (Peak) of (Y) Lliwedd (q.v.)
Llwybr Llanberis	The Llanberis Path
Llwybr Llyn Cwellyn	The Llyn Cwellyn (The Snowdon Ranger) Path
Llwybr Mwynwyr	The Miners' Track
Llwybr Pyg	The Pyg (q.v.) Track
Llwybr Rhyd-Ddu	The Rhyd-Ddu (The 'Beddgelert') Path
Llwybr Watcyn	The (Sir Edward) Watkin Path
Llwybr y Mûl	The Donkey Path
	The Pony Track
Llwyn-celyn	The Holly Bush
Llwyn Onn	The Grove (The Little Wood) of Ash Trees
Llwyn Peris	The Grove of (Saint) Peris
Llyn Bâch	The Lake (in a) Nook (a Secluded Corner)
	The Hook (The Hook-like) (Uncate) Lake
	The Small Lake
Llyn Cawellyn	The Osier Basket (The Wicker-work Basket) (The Creel) Lake (Lake)
	Cwellyn (q.v.)
	Quellyn (q.v.)

	Llyn Cwellyn (q.v.)
	Llyn Tarddennin (q.v.)
Llyn Coch	Red Lake
Llyn Cwellyn	Lake Cwellyn (q.v.)
Llyn Dinas	The Lake of the Hill Fort (Place) (Dinas Emrys) (q.v.)
Llyn Du'r Arddu	The Dark Lake of the Black Height (the Dark High Land)
Llyn Dwythwch	The Lake of (Cwm) Dwythwch (q.v.)
Llyn Ffynnon Las	The Lake of the Blue (Green) (Fountain-Head) Well
	Llyn y Ffynnon Las (q.v.)
	Llyn Glaslyn (q.v.)
	Glaslyn (q.v.)
Llyn Ffynnon-y-gwas	The Lake of the Fountain-Head of the Youth (the Lad)
	The Lake of the Well of Tranquillity (the Silence)
Llyn Glas[(1)]	The Blue Lake (in the Green Valley) (in Cwm Glas)
	The Grey Lake
	The Lake of the Stream
Llyn Glas[(2)]	The Green Lake (in Cwm Clogwyn)
Llyn Glas Mawr	The Great Blue-Green Lake
	Llyn Llydaw (q.v.)
Llyn Glaslyn	Glaslyn (q.v.) Lake
Llyn Gwynant	The Lake of (Nant) Gwynant (q.v.)
	The Lake of the White Brook
	The Lake of the White (Untainted) (Pure) (Unblemished) Little River
	The Lake of the White (Pure) (Holy) (Hallowed) (Revered) River Valley (The Perfect Valley Setting)
Llyn Llydaw	The Wide Lake
	The Lake (with an) (Extensive) Shore-Land

	The Lake of Scoriac Ash (Slaggy Material and Cinder-like Rock)
	The (Great Blue-Green) Lake (Llyn Glas Mawr, q.v.) now miscalled 'Brittany Lake' (see text)
Llyn Lockwood	The Lake of (the Angler) Lockwood
	Lockwood's Lake
	Llyn Penygwryd (q.v.)
Llyn Nadroedd	The Lake of Adders (the Nadders)
	The Lake of the Snakes
	The Lake of Serpents
	The Snakes' Pool
Llyn Padarn	The Lake of (Saint) Padarn (Saint Paternus)
Llyn Penygwryd	The Lake (at) Penygwryd (q.v.)
	Llyn Lockwood (q.v.)
Llyn Peris	The Lake of (Saint) Peris
Llyn Tarddennin	The Lake (Issuing Light)
	The (Light-sparkling Scintillant) Lake
	Llyn Cawellyn (q.v.)
Llyn Teyrn	The Lake of the Monarch (the Tyrant) (the Ruler) (King Arthur)
	(A Right Royal Fish-Pond)
Llyn y Ffynnon Las	The Lake of the Blue (Green) (Fountain-Head) Well
	Llyn Ffynnon Las (q.v.)
	Llyn Glaslyn (q.v.)
	Glaslyn (q.v.)
Llyn y Gader	The Lake of (Y) Gader (the Stronghold) (the Chair) (the Cradle)
Maen-bras	Large Stone (an erratic rock)
Maen-du'r Arddu	The Dark Stone of the Black Height (the Dark High Land)
Maen-llwyd	The Holy Stone (The Grey Stone)
Maen-llwyd-isaf	The Holy Stone (The Grey Stone) (Farm) the Lower

Maenhir[1]	Long-Stone (Monolith Marker Stone) (on the upper part of The Pyg Track, above Igam-Ogam, at Bwlch Glas)
Maenhir[2]	Long-Stone (Monolith Marker Stone) (at the upper part of The Watkin Path atop the diagonal trend to Bwlch Main)
Maesgwm	The Open-Field Valley The Valley of the (Upland) Plain
Moel Cynghorion	The Hill of the Counsels The Hill of the Counsellors The Councillors' Hill
Moel Eilio	The Hill of the Hue The Supporting Hill The Hill of (the Long Brow)
Moel yr Wyddfa	The Hill (The Mountain) of the Grave Snowdon (q.v.)
Mur-y-muriau	The Wall of Walls (The Enclosure of Enclosures) (a grassy terrace, a rampart said to be the site of a very holy place used by those necromantic priests of Celticism, the Old Druids) Murmarianau (q.v.)
Muriau Gwelltog	The Grassy Walls
Muriau'r Dre	Town Walls (The Walls of the Settlement) (an early Irish 'city' in Cwm Dyli)
Murmarianau	Moraines Rampart-Wall Terminations (Boundaries) Wall Mur-y-muriau (q.v.)
Nanhwynen	The Valley of Gwynen (Gwynan) (Gwynain) Nant Gwynen (q.v.) Nantgwynant (q.v.)
Nant Colwyn	The Valley of (the River) (Afon) Colwyn (q.v.) The Valley of Colwyn (the Great Shepherd of Brân)

	The Valley of the (Lively) Young Dog (the Pup) (the Whelp)
	The Valley of (the Grove in the Valley-Bottom)
Nant Cynnyd	The Brook of Gains
	The Brook of Increase (Growth) (Progress)
Nant Gwynant	Nantgwynant (q.v.)
Nant Gwynen	Nanhwynen (q.v.)
Nant Manllyn	The Brook of the Lake-Place
Nant Peris	The Valley of (Saint) Peris
	(The village of Nant Peris) (old Llanberis)
Nant y Betws	The Valley of the Oratory (the House of Prayer) (the Chapel-of-Ease) (Betws Garmon) (q.v.)
	The Valley of the Birch Grove (Bank)
Nant yr Aran	The Stream of (the High Place) (the Height) (the Rising Ground) (Yr Aran) (q.v.)
Nantgwynant	The Valley of Gwynen (Gwynan) (Gwynain) (Nanhwynen, q.v.)
	The Valley of the White Brook
	The Valley of the White (Untainted) (Pure) (Unblemished) Little River
Ochr y Bwlch	The Side (The Hill-Slope) of the Pass
Ogof Llanciau Eryri	The Cave of the (Brave) Young Men of Eryri (q.v.) (Snowdonia) (the Welsh Knights of Celtic King Arthur)
Pant yr Lluwchfa	The Hollow (and Rift) (The Couloir) of the Snow-Drift
Parc Hafod-y-llan	The Park (The Enclosure) (The Field) of Hafod-y-llan (q.v.)
Pen ar Lôn	The Top upon (over) (on) the Lane
	The End (of) the Lane
Pen Gallt-y-Llyn	The Head (The Top) (The End) of the (Wooded) Hill of the Lake

Pen-y-ceunant Isaf	The Top of the Ravine the Lower (House)
Pen-y-ceunant Uchaf	The Top of the Ravine the Higher (House)
Pen-y-Gwryd	Penygwryd (q.v.) (Hotel) (originally a small well-kept family ale-house, a remote wayside cottage, in the early nineteenth century, which became 'modernised' in 1847)
Pen-y-pass	The Top of the (Llanberis) Pass Pen-y-pass Hotel (Gorphwysfa) (q.v.) Gorffwysfa Peris (q.v.)
Penmaen-brith	The Grey Rock Headland The Mottled Rock Promontory (Elephant Rock)
Pentre-castell	The Village of the (by the) Castle (Castell Dolbadarn, q.v.)
Penygwryd	The Head (of) (the River) (Nant) y Gwryd (q.v., **Glyderau**) The Head (The Top) (The Pass) of the (Valorous) Bravery (the Manliness) (in Battle) The Top (of the Nantgwynant Pass at its entry into Dyffryn Mymbyr) of the Fathom (the Fathom-wide) (a Man's Length) (the Fathom-wide Out-stretched Arm-Reach) (of Sir Cai, one of King Arthur's Knights) (hence the name Penygwryd Cai, q.v.) Pen-y-Gwryd (q.v.)
Penygwryd Cai	Penygwryd (q.v.)
Perthi	The Hedges (The Bushes)
Pibell Dŵr	The Water-Pipe (The National Power Pipe-Line) (The Notorious and Ugly Out-of-Place Eyesore in this Otherwise Very Pretty Part of The Snowdonia National Park)

Plas-y-Coed	The House (The Manor) of the Wood
Plas-y-nant	The House (The Manor) of the Valley
	The House of the Brook
Plascwmllan	The House (The Slate-Quarry Manager's Residence) (in) (at the entrance to) Cwm Llan (q.v.) (in ruins) (ruined) (The walls are riddled and pock-marked with rifle-fire received during final military training of Commandos in preparation for the D-Day Landing, that massive Allied invasion on the Normandy beaches of France, in the Second World War, 6th June 1944. My Dad, a paratrooper, was there. In Caen, not Cwm Llan. The 6th Airborne Division. Pegasus. He trained on Salisbury Plain.
Plasisaf	The Lower House (of Plas-y-nant) (q.v.)
Pont Bethania	The Bridge (at) Bethania (q.v.)
Pont Cae'r gors	The Bridge of the Field of the Bog
Pont Goleugoed	The Bridge (at) (the Place of) Goleugoed (q.v.)
Pont y Gromlech	The Bridge of (Dinas y) Gromlech (q.v., **Glyderau**)
	The Bridge of the Cromlech (the Cromlech-like Upright Slabs) (the Megaliths) (the Columnar Cliffs)
Pyg (Track)	The Pig Track
	The Peak Track
	The Pitch Track
	The **Pen-y-G**wryd Track
	(The Capel Curig Path)
Quellyn	Cwellyn (q.v.)
Rhaeadrau	The Waterfalls (near The Watkin Path)
Rhaeadrau Cwm Merch	The Cwm Merch (q.v.) Cataracts
	The Waterfalls (in) the Valley of the (Young) Girl

149

Rhcilffordd Trên Bach	The (Narrow-Gauge) (Rack-&-Pinion)
Yr Wyddfa	Little-Train Railway of Snowdon
	(The Snowdon Mountain Railway)
Rhôs Boeth	Burnt (Hot) Upland-Moor
	The Sear Moor
Rhyd-Ddu	The Black (The Dark) River-Crossing
	(The Black Ford)
Salem	(a biblical name, (Jeru)Salem, given to
	the chapel and naming too the cluster of
	cottages here in Nant y Betws)
Snowdon	(a Norman word, Snaudun, Snawdon,
	meaning The Snow-Hill)
	Moel y Wyddfa (q.v.)
Tan-y-coed	Under-the-Wood
Tan-y-graig	Under-the-Rock
Tan-y-llyn	Below-the-Lake
Tro Eroplên	Aeroplane Bend
Tryfan	(a position on the ridge-way above Nant
	Peris which first affords a view across the
	col of an intervening shoulder of the
	Glyderau to the three-buttressed peak
	known as Tryfan (q.v., **Glyderau**))
Ty'n-y-ceunant	The Farm of the River-Gully
Ty'n-yr-aelgerth	The Farm of the Brow of the (Narrow)
	Hill (the Ridge)
	The Holding of the Enclosures' Edge
Tyn Weirglodd	The Farm of the Meadow
Wern	The Marsh
	The Place Where Alder Trees Grow
Wernlas-deg	The Fine Green Alder Trees Place
	Gwernlas-deg (q.v.)
Y Clogwyn	The Precipice
	The Cliff (Clogwyn Du'r Arddu, q.v.)
	(Station)
	Clogwyn (q.v.)

Y Cob	The Cob (The Embankment)
	The (Copper Miners') Causeway
Y Diffws	The Steep Slope (The Precipice)
	The Abyss
	The Desolate-Place
	(Y Diffwys)
Y Felin	The (dis-used and ruined) (Britannia) (Ore-Crushing) Mill (beside Llyn Llydaw)
Y Geuallt	The Hollow of the Hill
Y Grib Goch	Crib Goch (q.v.)
Y Lliwedd	The Shade
	The Swart
	The Livia (a Celtic proper name)
	The Appearance (The Aspect) of a Flood
	The Sight (The View) of a Flood
Y Pennant	The Valley Head
	The Brook End
Y Tylwyth Teg	The (Well-Meaning) Fair Family (of the Great Wisdom)
	The Beautiful (but damned) People
	The Mischievous (The Mischievously Evil) (The Dishonest and Cunning) Little (Welsh) Fairies
	(lakes, riverpools and submerged passages in mountain streams in our world are all thought to be gateways to and from their nether-land, Annwfn, The Celtic Under-World, hidden underground)
Y Wenallt	The White (Holy) (Hallowed) (Revered) (Fair) Wooded Hillside (Slope)
Ynys Ettws	The Ettws (Hettws) Holm
	Hetty's Island (Holm)
Yr Aelgerth	The Brow of the (Narrow) Hill (the Ridge)

151

	The Enclosures' Edge
Yr Aran	The Aran
	The (High Place)
	The (Height)
	The (Rising Ground)
Yr Wyddfa	The Tomb
	The Tumulus
	The Burial-Place
	The Grave
	The Mound
	The Monument
	The Eminence
	Yr Wyddfa Fawr (q.v.)
	(The Summit of Snowdon)
Yr Wyddfa Fawr	The Great Grave (Yr Wyddfa) (q.v.)
	The Great (The High) Eminence
	(The Great Summit of Snowdon)
Ysgar	The Rampart
	The Separate(d)
	Enemy
Ystrad	The Broad Valley
Ystrad-isaf	The Lower Strath

Appendices

Appendix 1: **Time-Table of One Hundred & Fifty-four Ascents**
A time-table of the author's (my own personal calendar of) 154 ascents of all the 3000-foot mountains of Wales

Appendix 2: **List of Good Lines of Ascent to Each Individual Mountain**
Glyderau
Carneddau
Snowdon Hills

Appendix 3: **List of Local Ordnance Survey Maps**
covering the Glyderau, Carneddau and Snowdon Hills, used for collection of many (500-odd) Welsh place-names appearing in **The Glossary**

Appendix 4: **A Select Bibliography for Walkers**
A list of interesting books about the locality as useful guides for walkers when planning and undertaking other walks in the Welsh 3000-foot mountains

Time-Table of One Hundred & Fifty-four Ascents
A time-table of the author's (my own personal calendar of) 154 ascents of all the 3000-foot mountains of Wales

3000-foot mountain and dates of ascents to the summit and number of ascents to date:

Glyder Fawr 8.7.1982, 3.8.1982, 30.8.1987, 22.5.1988, 29.5.1988, 15.8.1988, 19.6.1989, 27.8.1989, 24.4.1990, 5.9.1991, 17.5.1992,   **11**

Glyder Fach 8.7.1982, 3.8.1982, 29.5.1988, 15.8.1988, 19.6.1989, 24.4.1990, 27.5.1990, 22.7.1990, 25.7.1990, 5.9.1991, 17.5.1992,   **11**

Y Garn 7.6.1982, 7.8.1982, 14.8.1982, 22.5.1988, 3.7.1988, 18.7.1988, 3.9.1988, 4.6.1989, 14.3.1990, 4.9.1990, 8.8.1991, 26.3.1993,   **12**

Elidir Fawr 7.6.1982, 3.7.1988, 15.10.1988, 4.6.1989, 25.5.1990, 4.9.1990, 26.6.1992, 30.7.1992, 4.5.1993,   **9**

Tryfan 2.6.1982, 8.8.1982, 29.5.1988, 15.8.1988, 17.6.1989, 28.8.1989, 23.4.1990, 29.3.1991, 19.6.1993,   **9**

Carnedd Llywelyn 17.4.1982, 23.4.1988, 7.5.1988, 15.5.1988, 5.6.1988, 6.5.1989, 27.5.1989, 30.9.1989, 31.3.1990, 1.8.1990, 7.9.1991, 28.7.1992,   **12**

Carnedd Dafydd 10.5.1982, 7.5.1988, 5.6.1988, 8.8.1988, 30.10.1988, 6.5.1989, 30.9.1989, 18.3.1990, 30.4.1990, 8.5.1991, 12.6.1992,   **11**

Pen yr Ole-wen 10.5.1982, 18.7.1982, 7.5.1988, 5.6.1988, 8.8.1988, 30.10.1988, 6.5.1989, 30.9.1989, 18.3.1990, 8.5.1991, 12.6.1992, 29.4.1993,   **12**

Foel Grach 17.4.1982, 15.5.1988, 5.6.1988, 27.5.1989, 30.9.1989, 3.5.1990, 21.5.1990, 18.8.1991, 7.9.1991,   **9**

Yr Elen 4.1982, 23.4.1988, 27.5.1989, 16.7.1989, 30.4.1990, 22.5.1990, 1.8.1990, 28.7.1992, **8**

Foel-fras 17.4.1982, 15.5.1988, 20.5.1989, 3.5.1990, 26.5.1992, 22.7.1992, **6**

Garnedd Uchaf 17.4.1982, 5.6.1988, 20.5.1989, 27.5.1989, 3.5.1990, 18.8.1991, 7.9.1991, 26.5.1992, **8**

Snowdon 13.1.1982, 13.6.1988, 20.6.1988, 7.9.1988, 14.10.1988, 11.3.1989, (28.5.1989) (flight), (24.6.1989) (railway), 29.6.1989, 3.9.1989, 13.1.1990, 18.7.1990, 10.9.1990, 27.4.1991, 15.5.1992, 25.3.1993, 27.4.1993, 7.5.1993, **16**

Garnedd Ugain 7.9.1988, (28.5.1989) (flight), 29.6.1989, 3.9.1989, 2.5.1990, 18.7.1990, 24.7.1990, 31.7.1990, 14.8.1991, 3.9.1991, 15.5.1992, 22.5.1992, 27.4.1993, **12**

Crib Goch 7.9.1988, (28.5.1989) (flight), 2.5.1990, 18.7.1990, 14.8.1991, 3.9.1991, 22.5.1992, 27.4.1993, 5.5.1993, **8**

number of ascents to the Snowdonian summits up to the end of 1993: **154**

Glyderau

Glyder Fawr (3279 feet)
Pen Llyn Ogwen — Afon Idwal — entrance into Cwm Idwal at Llyn Idwal's outflow — east shore's path to wall — ascend above Clogwyn y Tarw (the adventurous from here will find a contouring path above the Sub-Cneifion Rib into lower Cwm Cneifion and work a way up the blunt north ridge to The Upper Cliff and then walk direct to **Glyder Fawr**, but others who baulk at the prospect of Seniors' Ridge will instead go via Y Gribin arguing to themselves that this is the more scenic route anyway) — Y Gribin — the rim of Blaen Cwm Cneifion — **Glyder Fawr** (only 999 metres in height, but never mind, your head at least will overtop the 1000-metre mark!) — south(wards) then south-east to keep on the courtesy (permissive) path (red marker spots (dots) on rocks) (rockshelf at spot height 646m) — arm of Cwmffynnon — Pen-y-pass

Glyder Fach (3262 feet)
Llyn Ogwen — Nant Bochlwyd — entrance into Cwm Bochlwyd at Llyn Bochlwyd's outflow — Bwlch Tryfan — The Bristly Ridge (The North East Ridge of Glyder Fach) — Y Gwyliwr — **Glyder Fach** — Castell y Gwynt — Bwlch y Ddwy-Glyder — Y Gribin — Llyn Bochlwyd's outflow — Nant Bochlwyd — Llyn Ogwen

Llyn Penygwryd — The Miners' Path (a rocky trackway, a rough track home, worn out of the mountain by the hobnailed abrasion and the ring and clatter of a generation of miners' work-boots returning home to Bethesda at the weekend to stay with their families and to go to chapel on Sunday the Sabbath) (copper miners, don't you know, were worn out at the age of forty) —

Bwlch Caseg-fraith — edge overlooking into Cwm Tryfan — the top of The Bristly Ridge — Y Gwyliwr — **Glyder Fach** — Castell y Gwynt (from the peak of this spiky castlet, the contiguous vicinity of the external outward surface of The Glyders often lay exposed to my view) — path descending below Waun Gron — Bwlch Dwyglydion (through a treacherous terrain of ericaceous shrubs, ling (*Calluna vulgaris*), bell heather (*Erica cinerea*), cross-leaved heath (*Erica tetralix*) and bilberry (*Vaccinium myrtillus*) (Bwlch Dwyglydion is a slithery slope of deceitful heather, bracken and boulder) (*gliddery* is the Yorkshire expression for slippery) — Cwmffynnon — rock outcrop at spot height 379m (three quick dives, naked, into the river-pool!) — stream and waterfalls to Llyn Penygwryd

Y Garn (3104 feet)
Pen Llyn Ogwen — Pen y Benglog — the west end of the north beach of Llyn Idwal — Nant (careful not to step on butterworts (*Pinguicula vulgaris*) and sundews (*Drosera rotundifolia*) hereabouts: they are carnivorous) Clyd — entrance into Cwm Clyd — Llyn Clyd — Llyn Clyd Bach — north east ridge (with a remarkable final staircase of slate spikes to ascend) — **Y Garn** — south rim of Cwm Clyd — Castell y Geifr — keep to the edge to Cneifion Duon above Clogwyn y Gogledd also called Clogwyn y Geifr (here, appropriately, I once came close to a goat, a shaggy brown feral goat, *Capra hircus*, and we, Aries and Capricorn, eyed each other) (the wild goat survives today within the hircine genes of the several feral groups of local mountain goats (kids at heel, billies alert) as a reminder of the once great herds of milking goats which once played an important part in the transhumance farming of Snowdonia, that seasonal migration of stock and hill-farmer between *hendre* and *hafod*) — the top of Twll Du (look into the cleft at the exit into Twll Du) (your photograph of the prospect between the cliffs of this cleft, with Llyn Idwal and Llyn Ogwen a thousand feet below and Carnedds in the distance, will resemble hundreds of others taken from this same grassy bank on which you now stand but nevertheless it is the best photographic souvenir of this walk

and it will imprint upon you a memory that will remain when much
else in life is forgotten) (the stream entering Twll Du is from Llyn y
Cŵn, not far away) — keep to cliff edge south-east — Llwybr y
Carw (above Clogwyn y De) — rocks at waterfall at entrance into
Twll Du — path down into (west) Cwm Idwal — west shore and
(insectivorous plants abound hereabouts) the north beach of Llyn
Idwal — Llyn Idwal's outflow — Afon Idwal (wheatears, rumps
conspicuously white, flit about: 'wheatears', by the way, is a
sophism for white-arses; *Oenanthe oenanthe*) — Pen Llyn Ogwen

Elidir Fawr (3030 feet)

Nant Ffrancon old road (heading toward the headwall of The
Glyders here is like walking toward and straight into that classic J.
Arthur Dixon picture-postcard 'Tryfan seen from the old road,
Nant Ffrancon Valley, Gwynedd') above Blaen-y-nant farm —
follow stream from Cwm Cywion — turn right onto the ridge above
The Mushroom Garden (look down at the emergent stumps and
caps and columns and pillars of rock growing phycomycete-like
out of, that's why it's called, The Mushroom Garden below) — Y
Llymllwyd — Foel-goch — Bwlch y Brecan — Bwlch y Marchlyn
— **Elidir Fawr** — Bwlch Melynwyn — south(ward) spur to wall —
footbridge (a single hand-rail bridge) over Afon Dudodyn — Fron-
rhedyn — Nant Peris village

Nant Ffrancon old road (in part in places the old cart-track and
1792 stage-coach road) at Tai-newyddion — wall — eastern arm of
Cwm Graianog (a neat semi-circular rim, a crescent-shaped
moraine, called, in Welsh, The Maiden's Arm) — south ridge
looking across at The Corrugated Slabs of Cwm Graianog —
Carnedd y Filiast — Mynydd Perfedd — Bwlch y Marchlyn —
Elidir Fawr — Bwlch y Marchlyn — (a) Bwlch y Brecan — Cwm
Bual (below Foel-goch & Yr Esgair) — contour into Cwm-coch —
sheep-walk to wall below The Mushroom Garden — Yr Hafod at
the head of the Nant Ffrancon old road, (b) Bwlch y Brecan —
Llwybr yr Offeiriad (The Priest's Path) (in places) into Cwm Bual
— stream and waterfalls — Nant Ffrancon old road — Maes
Caradog farm — Tai-newyddion, (c) Bwlch y Brecan — Cwm

Perfedd below Mynydd Perfedd — eastern arm of Cwm Graianog — wall — Tai-newyddion, or (d) Mynydd Perfedd — Carnedd y Filiast — immediately above The Corrugated Slabs — The North Edge of Cwm Graianog (**careful!**) — northeastern arm — Tai-newyddion

Tryfan (3010 feet)

Gwern Gof Uchaf farm — past Tryfan Bach — The Heather Terrace — **Tryfan** — Far South Peak — Bwlch Tryfan — The Miners' Path only a short distance, to the peat pools on your left, and here descend into Cwm Tryfan — follow the course of Nant Gwern y Gof — Gwern Gof Uchaf farm

Gwern Gof Uchaf farm — past Tryfan Bach — The North Ridge — **Tryfan** (*don't* recklessly attempt a standing jump from Stone to Stone and back) — Far South Peak — Bwlch Tryfan — The Miners' Path — Bwlch Caseg-fraith — Llyn y Caseg-fraith — Drws Nodded — Braich y Ddeugwm — Gwern Gof Isaf farm (where many a lambkin has commenced its bleating) — old track in Nant y Benglog (part of the 1805 Capel Curig Turnpike Trust toll road, a stage-coach and mail-coach road) back to Gwern Gof Uchaf farm

Carneddau

Carnedd Llywelyn (3485 feet)

Gwern Gof Isaf farm — cross the road (The 1818 Shrewsbury to Bangor Ferry Turnpike Trust toll road) (Thomas Telford's London to Holyhead (Caergybi & Ireland) 1830s Highway) (The A5) — access road (a National Rivers' Authority access road to a reservoir, Ffynnon Llugwy) — Ffynnon Llugwy's outflow — ascend grass slopes by boulders to arrive on the broad ridge above Craig y Llyn — west on this south arm of Cwm Llugwy, to wall above Creigiau Hirion — edge of Cwm Llugwy's ridge — the junction of three ridges — Bwlch Cyfrwy-drum — **Carnedd**

Llywelyn — east arm — Penywaun-wen — at the head of Craig yr Ysfa to look into the depths of Cwm Eigiau — Bwlch Eryl Farchog — Pen yr Helgi Du — Y Braich — leat (carrying Afon Llugwy's water eastward to Llyn Cowlyd) — Tal-y-braich-uchaf farm — cross (with care!) The A5 — Helyg (Willows) (The Hut of The Climbers' Club) — Gwern Gof Isaf farm

Carnedd Dafydd (3423 feet)

Gwernydd — (Bangor) Water Wks — cross Afon Cenllusg at Gwern-Saeson-fawr — path (vague and boggy at first) above Afon Llafar — Mynydd Du — Cwm Llafar's west ridge edge — Foel Meirch — **Carnedd Dafydd** — on the brink of Cefn Ysgolion Duon — the junction of three ridges — halfway across the col at Bwlch Cyfrwy-drum — down to Nant Fach springs — Nant Fach — confluences of streams below Cwm Glas Bach forming the Afon Llafar (the threat of the dark ledges of The Black Ladders is behind you) (Ysgolion Duon is 'The most horrid precipice that thought can conceive', according to Thomas Pennant in 1773 and Terence Ogmore Batt in 1993) — a leisurely stroll on the path above the Afon Llafar (in the glorious sunshine of this summer's day mid-afternoon sun) down Cwm Pen-llafar (the river meanders, brown trout leap in the heat) — return to Gwernydd — Gerlan

Pen yr Ole-wen (3211 feet)

Pont Pen y Benglog — direct (an unrelentingly arduous ascent) to **Pen yr Ole-wen** — Bwlch yr Ole Wen (Carnedd Dafydd is easily attained from here but beware, because the wind sometimes rages across the ridge from Bwlch yr Ole Wen to Carnedd Fach above Cwm Lloer at this let's call it Cefn y Gwynt. I have seen walkers with heavy rucsacs bodily lifted by the strength of the wind that blows here, and tumbled over) — Braich Ty Du — Carreg Frân — Braich Ty Du wall — descend to path high above Ty'n-y-maes farm — path (part of The Priest's Path, Llwybr yr Offeiriad) diagonally back down to Tŷ Gwyn farm — cross with care The A5 — keep to the footpath across the meadow — footbridge over Afon Ogwen — Nant Ffrancon old road — Pentre farm — above and a short way beyond Blaen-y-nant farm — cut across to the true left bank of boulders at Rhaeadr Ogwen — Rhaeadr Ogwen — Pont Pen y Benglog

Pont Tal y Llyn — Glan Dena — wall with style at Tal y Llyn Ogwen farm — follow Afon Lloer up — east arm of Yr Ole Wen — keep close to edge above Cwm Lloer looking down on sparkling Ffynnon Lloer — **Pen yr Ole-wen** — direct descent — Pont Pen y Benglog — rough path (a remnant of the pre-1792 pack-horse track) near the north shore of Llyn Ogwen — pass by above Tal y Llyn Ogwen farm — Glan Dena — Pont Tal y Llyn (No. This walk is much better accomplished in the reverse direction. Start at Pont Pen y Benglog. Sorry about that.)

Foel Grach (3202 feet)

The A5 in Nant y Benglog between Gwern Gof Isaf farm and Helyg at the entrance to the National Rivers' Authority access road — path east of Ffynnon Llugwy — Bwlch Eryl Farchog — the head of Craig yr Ysfa to look into the depths of Cwm Eigiau — Penywaun-wen — Carnedd Llywelyn — north arm — the innominate rock outcrop (let's call it Castell, q.v.) at Gwaun y Garnedd — **Foel Grach** — Garnedd Uchaf — Yr Aryg — Bera Bach — Drosgl — hillside at source of Afon Ffrydlas — Afon Ffrydlas — Ffos Rhufeiniaid — Bwlch ym Mhwll-le — Rachub

Road above Tal-y-bont in the Vale of Conwy (up a 1-in-2 steep and winding lane in first gear, this is perilous alpine motoring!) into the Carneddau mountains to park at the roadhead not far from Llyn Eigiau near Trasbwll — track toward Clogwynyreryr — skirt Cerrig Cochion — Maeneira (ruin) — Afon Dulyn — path (vague and very boggy at first) into Pant y Griafolen — Dulyn's outflow (photograph the great cliff of Craig y Dulyn, The Crag of Dulyn The Black Lake) — direct (scramble up a left-hand stream-bed of Craig y Dulyn cliffs, and, at the edge of nowhere in the middle of nowhere, head straight across a featureless moor (this is *terra incognita*) to **Foel Grach** — descend south then eastwards toward Gledrffordd — the eastmost tributary of Afon Eigiau — halt opposite Craig yr Ysfa cliffs — Cwm Eigiau path — Llyn Eigiau track — return to your parking place at the remote roadhead

Yr Elen (3152 feet)

Ciltwllan — quarry track below Y Garth — sheep enclosures ('Settlement') — find and follow the (dried-up) leat at the bases of Drosgl & Bera Bach & Yr Aryg in an arc into Cwm Afon Caseg — Afon Wen — quarry track below Carreg y Gath — entrance to Cwm Bychan — (true) left bank of Afon Caseg (the right is absolutely soakingly soggy and cannot be crossed without profanity) — Cwm Caseg (See! A wild mare and her foal!) — Ffynnon Caseg — the unnamed north-east Ridge of Dragon's Teeth Rocks (Crib y Ddanned Draig) (Crib y Creigiau'r Ddanned Draig) — **Yr Elen** — Foel Ganol — Braich y Brysgyll — Cors Gwaun y Gwiail — cross Afon Caseg — quarry track below Y Garth — Ciltwllan

Foel-fras (3091 feet)

Rachub — Bwlch ym Mhwll-le — quarry track and path(s) below Gyrn — (first) trackway leading to Drosgl's western shoulder — Drosgl — Bera Bach — Yr Aryg — Garnedd Uchaf — **Foel-fras** — return to broad col — contour path to avoid Garnedd Uchaf again — Yr Aryg — Bera Mawr — descend boulders and bilberries of Bera Mawr's north ridge to The Windy Gap — west then north on broad shoulder (through stone hut circles, very desirable residences with outstanding views, in pre-historic times) to overlook Rhaeadr-fawr (Aber Falls) — a remarkable cliff edge sheep-walk looking toward (here is a seldom-seen sight well worth this long pilgrimage) Rhaeadr-bach (The Prettiest-looking Waterfall in North Wales) — cross Afon Rhaeadr-bach a short distance back from the fall — path between Drosgl and Moel Wnion heading for Gyrn — peat hags (pools) — path(s) below Gyrn — track to Bwlch ym Mhwll-le — back to Rachub

Bont Newydd (less than a mile from the village of Aber) (Abergwyngregyn) — Nant (Nant Rhaeadr) — a rising track at the edge of a forest (and into a pine plantation) — emerge and cross diagonally the scree below Marian Rhaeadr-fawr — a position above Rhaeadr-fawr (Aber Falls) — Afon Goch — waterfall at entrance into upper Cwm yr Afon Goch — Llwydmor — **Foel-fras** — Garnedd Uchaf — Yr Aryg — Bera Bach — Bera Mawr — Bera Mawr's (bouldery and bilberry) north ridge — Afon Goch at waterfall at entrance into upper Cwm yr Afon Goch — follow the course of Afon Goch — position above Rhaeadr-fawr (Aber Falls) — cross the scree — walk to boulders at the base of The Very Spectacular Aber Falls (Rhaeadr-fawr) — take the tourists' track back, down The Oak-wooded Valley — Bont Newydd (The 'New' Bridge) (Look at the rivering waters under the bridge. This is a river that changes its name. On the seaward side of the bridge it flows out as Afon Aber, an alias for Afon Rhaeadr-fawr on the other (upstream) side. And, before the same river cascades and falls as The Great Waterfall (Aber Falls), Afon Aber alias Afon Rhaeadr-fawr is actually then alias the original Afon Goch!)

Garnedd Uchaf (3038 feet)
This insignificant 'summit' has already been 'ascended' three times in passing (see under **Foel Grach** and **Foel-fras** walks)

Snowdon Hills

Snowdon (3559 feet)
There are six conventional ways to walk by path to the summit of Snowdon: Llwybr Llanberis (The Llanberis Path), Llwybr Llyn Cwellyn (The Llyn Cwellyn (The Snowdon Ranger) Path), Llwybr Rhyd-Ddu (The Rhyd-Ddu (The 'Beddgelert') Path), Llwybr Watcyn (The Watkin Path, The Path of Sir Edward Watkin, Bart., a rich and influential railway-owner and Liberal MP), Llwybr Mwynwyr (The Miners' Track) and Llwybr Pyg (The Pyg Track). Llwybr y Mûl (The Donkey Path, The Pony Track), a connection across and combination in part of The Miners' Track and The Pyg Track, is rarely followed by walkers (or donkeys) these days.

Pen-y-pass — a position between The Hummocks of The Horns and the edge of Craig Llyn Teyrn — The Copper Miners' Causeway (Y Cob) to cut across Llyn Llydaw — The Miners' Track — Glaslyn — The Pyg Track — The Gabions and The Zig-Zag (Igam-Ogam) — Maenhir[1] at Bwlch Glas — **Snowdon** — return to Maenhir[1] at Bwlch Glas — The Zag-Zig (Ogam-Igam) and The Gabions — The Pyg Track — Bwlch y Moch — unnamed summit (609m) — The Hummocks of The Horns — Pen-y-pass

Pen-y-pass — Bwlch y Moch — The Pyg Track — The Gabions and The Zig-Zag — Maenhir[1] at Bwlch Glas — **Snowdon** — Bwlch Main — south by edge of Clogwyn Du above Cwm Tregalan — Allt Maenderyn — Bwlch Cwm Llan — Yr Aran — Craig Wen — head more or less just left of Hebog (keep close to walls and remain unobserved on this trespassing descent) (Cocyn Perthi to Beudy Ysgubor to end up on the roadway to Gwernlas-deg) — The A4085 in Nant Colwyn — the village of Beddgelert

Llyn Cwellyn — (The Llyn Cwellyn (The Snowdon Ranger) Path) Llwyn Onn — Bwlch Cwm Brwynog — the edge of Clogwyn Du'r Arddu looking down on Llyn Du'r Arddu — Bwlch Glas — **Snowdon** — Bwlch Main — Llechog (The Rhyd Ddu (The 'Beddgelert') Path) — Rhôs Boeth — Pen ar Lôn — Rhyd-Ddu (Rhyd-Ddu car park was once the station yard of the narrow-gauge Welsh Highland Railway's South Snowdon Station)

Llanberis — Cader Ellyll — Derlwyn (The Nant Peris Ridge Way) — Tryfan — Llechog — Clogwyn Station (Rheilffordd Trên Bach Yr Wyddfa) (look down with trepidation into the depth of Cwm Hetiau and hold on to your hat!) — The Llanberis Path — **Snowdon** — back to Bwlch Glas — Garnedd Ugain — Gyrn Lâs — contour across and cross the rack & pinion track before Clogwyn Station — descend by a brook north of Clogwyn Coch — encircle Llyn Du'r Arddu — return to the climbers' path — The Llanberis Path — an easy afternoon stroll back to Llanberis

Pen-y-pass — Bwlch y Moch — The East Ridge of (my Gramps and Grandad accompany me and make my legs strong) Crib Goch — The Three Pinnacles — Bwlch Coch — Crib y Ddysgl —

Garnedd Ugain — Bwlch Glas — **Snowdon** — Maenhir[2] — The
Watkin Path — Bwlch y Saethau — The Edge (look down the
length of Llyn Llydaw) — Bwlch Ciliau — Y Lliwedd west peak —
Y Lliwedd east peak — Lliwedd Bach — Llyn Llydaw at its (very
diminished) outflow into Cwm Dyli — Cwt Falf — The
Hummocks of The Horns (or, but this is cheating, Cwt Falf — The
Miners' Track) — Pen-y-pass (This is **The Snowdon Horseshoe**
walk, the best traverse in Wales, described more fully in outline in
the **Introduction**, q.v.)

Garnedd Ugain (3495 feet)
The Llanberis Pass near Blaen-y-nant — path up into Cwm Glas
Mawr — Llyn Glas — Cwm Uchaf — Bwlch Coch — Crib y
Ddysgl — **Garnedd Ugain** — Gyrn Lâs — Cwm Glas — Llyn Bâch
— Cwm Glas Mawr — Blaen-y-nant — The Llanberis Pass

Pen-y-pass — first ½ mile of The Pyg Track — Craig Fach — (there
is a path) Cwm Beudy Mawr — ascend the shoulder between The
North Ridge of Crib Goch and Dinas Mot — contour across this
lonely place to Llyn Glas — the columnar base of Clogwyn y Person
(you are about to enter the lost valley of Cwm Glas) — Llyn Bâch —
Gyrn Lâs — ascend due south at the west edge of Cwm Glas cliffs
— **Garnedd Ugain** — Maenhir[1] at Bwlch Glas — The Zag-Zig
(Ogam-Igam) and The Gabions — down to Glaslyn — Afon
Glaslyn — Llyn Llydaw (swim[1]) — path along the south shore of
Llyn Llydaw (swim[2]) — Cwt Falf — The Smooth Rock Outcrop
at The North 'Pool' of Llyn Llydaw cut off by The Causeway (dive
in three times in this deep blue lagoon) (swim[3]) — The
Hummocks of The Horns — Pen-y-pass

Garnedd Ugain is ascended in traversing **The Snowdon
Horseshoe** and elsewhere twice again (see under **Snowdon** and
Crib Goch)

Crib Goch (3029 feet)
Pen-y-pass — first ½ mile of The Pyg Track — Craig Fach — (an

occasional cairn marks the direction of the path) Cwm Beudy Mawr — ascend the shoulder well above Dinas Mot cliffs — The North (only attempt on a wind-still day) Ridge — **Crib Goch** — The Three Pinnacles — Bwlch Coch — Cwm Uchaf — skirt the ruddy scree — shoulder above Dinas Mot — Cwm Beudy Mawr (find the path) — Craig Fach — last ½ mile along The Pyg Track — the car park at Pen-y-pass

Pen-y-pass — Bwlch y Moch — The East Ridge — **Crib Goch** — The Three Pinnacles — Bwlch Coch — Crib y Ddysgl — Garnedd Ugain — west edge of Cwm Glas — Gyrn Lâs — Clogwyn Station — Llechog (The Nant Peris Ridge Way) — Tryfan — Derlwyn — Cader Ellyll — stroll (strut) into the town of Llanberis

Crib Goch is the first summit ascended in the six-hour anti-clockwise circuit of **The Snowdon Horseshoe** (see under **Snowdon** above)

Appendix 3:
List of Local Ordnance Survey Maps
covering the Glyderau, Carneddau and Snowdon Hills, used for collection of many (500-odd) Welsh place-names appearing in **The Glossary**

Snowdonia National Park Half-Inch Map (contoured in feet) (1:126 720) made and published by the Ordnance Survey, Southampton (Crown copyright 1979)

Caernarfon & Bangor Landranger Series Sheet 115 (1:50 000) made and published by the Ordnance Survey, Southampton (Crown copyright 1974)

Snowdon & surrounding area (Yr Wyddfa) Landranger Series Sheet 115 (1:50 000) made and published by the Ordnance Survey, Southampton (Crown copyright 1991)

Bethesda (Gwynedd) Pathfinder Series Sheet SH 66/76 (1:25 000) made and published by the Ordnance Survey, Southampton (Crown copyright 1980)

Snowdon & Betws-y-Coed Pathfinder Series Sheet SH 65/75 (1:25 000) made and published by the Ordnance Survey, Southampton (Crown copyright 1980)

Snowdonia National Park — Conwy Valley Outdoor Leisure Map (1:25 000) (contoured in feet) made and published by the Ordnance Survey, Southampton (Crown copyright 1977)

Snowdonia National Park — Snowdon Outdoor Leisure Map (1:25 000) (contoured in feet) made and published by the Ordnance Survey, Southampton (Crown copyright 1977)

Snowdonia — Snowdon area (Eryri: ardal yr Wyddfa) Outdoor Leisure Map 17 (1:25 000) made and published by the Ordnance Survey, Southampton (Crown copyright 1984)

Snowdonia: Snowdon & Conwy Valley areas (Eryri: ardal yr Wyddfa a Dyffryn Conwy) Outdoor Leisure Map 17 (1:25 000) made and published by the Ordnance Survey, Southampton (Crown copyright 1992)

Appendix 4:
A Select Bibliography for Walkers

A list of interesting books about the locality as useful guides for walkers when planning and undertaking other walks in the Welsh 3000-foot mountains

Addison, K. (1988): *The Ice Age in Snowdonia. The Ice Age in Y Glyderau and Nant Ffrancon*. K. & M.K. Addison, Broseley, Shropshire.

Allen, R. (1993): *On Foot in Snowdonia: The Best Hill Walks and Scrambles from Cadair Idris to the Carneddau*. Michael Joseph, London.

Anon. (1990): *Getting to know Gwynedd: Information for Newcomers*. (Produced by members of PONT Gwynedd). Gwasg Ffrancon, Bethesda, Gwynedd.

Ashton, S. (1980): *Scrambles in Snowdonia*. Cicerone Press, Cumbria (second edition 1992).

Ashton, S. (1988): *Hill Walking in Snowdonia*. Cicerone Press, Cumbria.

Barber, C. (1986): *The Romance of The Welsh Mountains. An anthology of climbers' tales and walkers' ways*. Blorenge Books, Abergavenny, Gwent.

Batt, T. (1991): *Not The Snowdon Horseshoe Again*. (unpublished typescript, 7pp).

Carr, H.R.C. and Lister, G.A. (eds.) (1925): *The Mountains of Snowdonia (in History, The Sciences, Literature and Sport)*. Crosby Lockwood & Son Ltd, London (second edition 1948).

Condry, W. (1987): *Snowdonia*. David & Charles, Newton Abbot, Devon.

Davies, J. (1993): *The Welsh Language*. University of Wales Press, Cardiff.

Doylerush, E. (1985): *No Landing Place. A guide to aircraft crashes in Snowdonia*. Midland Counties Publications (Aerophile) Ltd., Leicester.

Grisedale, J.O. (1989): *Why Snowdon is A Danger*. Winter Post (Llanberis Mountain Rescue Team warning leaflet). Gwasg Ffrancon, Bethesda, Gwynedd.

Helliwell, R. (1946): *The Idwal Log. The Youth Hostellers' guide to rambles and scrambles and matters of local interest in the Ogwen District*. Merseyside Youth Hostels Ltd., Birkenhead (third edition 1974).

Hinson, D. (1987): *Walks in the Snowdonia Mountains*. Gwasg Carreg Gwalch, Capel Garmon, Llanrwst, Gwynedd.

Hubback, D. (1987): *Time and the Valley: The Past, Present and Future of the Upper Ogwen Valley*. Gwasg Carreg Gwalch, Capel Garmon, Llanrwst, Gwynedd.

Jones, J. (1983): *The Lakes of North Wales*. Whittet Books Ltd., London.

Jones, R. (1992): *The Complete Guide to Snowdon: Yr Wyddfa*. Gwasg Carreg Gwalch, Capel Garmon, Llanrwst, Gwynedd.

Ll.J. (Lloyd-Jones), E. (1935): *A Night on The Carnedds: A Tale of The Hills*. Phillipson and Golder Ltd., Chester.

Marsh, T. (1985): *The Mountains of Wales. A walker's guide to the 600-metre summits*. Hodder and Stoughton, London.

Maslen-Jones, R. (1993): *Countdown to Rescue*. The Ernest Press, Holyhead, Gwynedd.

Mulholland, H. (1982): *Guide to Wales' 3000-foot Mountains. The Welsh Munros*. Mulholland-Wirral, Little Neston, South Wirral.

Nuttall, J. and Nuttall, A. (1989): *The Mountains of England and Wales. Volume 1: Wales*. Cicerone Press, Cumbria.

Pardoe, H.S. and Thomas, B.A. (1992): *Snowdon's Plants Since The Glaciers: A Vegetational History*. National Museum of Wales, Cardiff.

Poucher, W.A. (1962): *The Welsh Peaks. A pictorial guide to walking in this region and to the safe ascent of its principal mountain groups, with 250 photographs by the author, 15 maps and 56 routes*. Constable and Company Ltd., London (seventh edition 1979).

Rowland, E.G. (1951): *Hill Walking in Snowdonia. Fifty 2000 foot peaks in The Snowdonia National Park*. Camping and Open Air Press Ltd., 38 Grosvenor Gardens, London SW1.

Rowland, E.G. (1956): *The Ascent of Snowdon. The six classic routes up Snowdon*. Cicerone Press, Cumbria (fifth edition 1975).

Senior, M. (1987): *Portrait of North Wales*. Gwasg Carreg Gwalch, Capel Garmon, Llanrwst, Gwynedd.

Thomas, R.S. (1992): *Cymru or Wales? (A personal essay in the* changing Wales *series. Series editor: Meic Stephens)*. J.D. Lewis and Sons Ltd., Gomer Press, Llandysul, Dyfed.

THE MOUNTAIN WALKER'S GUIDE TO WALES

by Colin Adams

192 pages: Map: ISBN: 0-86381-154-X; Price: £6.90 including plastic protective cover

- describes 100 routes of varying lengths and difficulty, from gentle strolls to tough excursions which covers 200 Welsh peaks
- contains something suitable for every category of walker
- includes virtually every mountain summit in Wales, many of which are represented in a guide for the first time
- covers every mountain group in Wales
- gives practical advice about safety and equipment
- provides fascinating geological, historical and general interest facts

SNOWDONIA, A HISTORICAL ANTHOLOGY

by David Kirk

Price: £5.95

Snowdonia, a Historical Anthology draws from the observations of nearly 60 writers across 1,800 years to portray the people and landscape of one of the most beautiful regions of Europe.

From the Roman historian Tacitus in the 1st century AD through Nennius, Gerald de Barri, Thomas Pennant, William Bingley and a host of later visitors, a picture emerges of change, resilience and continuity.

The result is both a fascinating history and a practical guidebook as almost everything described can still be explored and enjoyed.

A GUIDE TO WELSH PLACE-NAMES
by Anthony Lias
Price: £3.50

The great majority of Welsh place-names, unlike English ones, make very good sense in their present-day forms — provided, of course, that you know something about Welsh itself!

This book is specifically designed to reduce the language problem to a minimum. Drawing on some 500 place-name examples, the author gives their meanings and analyses their different constructions in a simple and concise way; he also sketches in the linguistic and historical background to Welsh names, as well as pinpointing some of the varied human interests that lie behind them (nor are Brythonic-based names in England overlooked).

Although primarily a guide, the book will — ideally — assist readers to find their own way around the Welsh place-name field.

Readers' notes and observations . . .

Readers' notes and observations . . .

Readers' notes and observations . . .

Readers' notes and observations . . .

Readers' notes and observations . . .

Walkers on The Pyg Track usually ignore the unnamed 609-metre summit at grid reference 635553 indifferently by-passed behind them above Bwlch y Moch. The wizard Gwydion once passed this way with King Pryderi's Stolen Swine. Pigs in Welsh is moch. This is The Pig Track. This rock is **Craig Moch**.

Photographs

All photographs reproduced in the text and that used on the cover, with the exception of the photographs on page 89 (upper photograph), page 91, page 95 (Jacqueline Ehlen) and page 177 (Colin Brown), were taken by the author (Terence Ogmore Batt), and copyright of all these photographs is held by us.

Publishers Note:
The very nature of this work requires constant revision, alteration, amendment, updating and readjustment by the author and already, even before going to press (1994), a revised and illustrated edition (planned in preparation) is in progress.